Blazing Tales
'the river exe-pedition'

A combined arts project with
mixed-heritage families in Devon

Contrary to popular perception, mixed race families in Britain are not – and never have been – confined to an urban, inner-city experience, as Sara Hurley so excellently highlights in the wonderful Blazing Tales: 'the river exe-pedition'. In this creative and thought-provoking book, Hurley explores the ways in which place and space shape our sense of self and belonging through a focus on the overlooked experience of racial mixing and mixedness in rural Britain. Drawing on a fascinating and eclectic combined arts project undertaken with mixed racial families in Devon, Blazing Tales takes a fresh and challenging look at what it means to be – and be seen to be - part of a mixed race family beyond the British city.

Containing a wealth of material in the form of local history, interviews, workshop activities and evaluations, Hurley's book provides not only key first hand insights into rural mixed race family life, but also thoughtful guidance on conducting creative workshops with families generally.

Trailbreaking, reflective and inspirational, Blazing Tales make a fantastic contribution to the existing literature on mixed race families and is essential reading for academics, policy-makers, practitioners and educators who are looking for a refreshing and stimulating change of focus and thinking about their understandings of and work with mixed race families in Britain.

Dr Chamion Caballero, *Senior Research Fellow, Weeks Centre for Social and Policy Research, London South Bank University*

In this book Sara Hurley and Malcolm Learmonth give a moving and honest account of inspirational work in the outdoors that receives far too little, and then often sensational, attention. It bursts with ideas and insights while emphasizing the critical importance of building relationships wherever you live or arrive.

The descriptions of practice are evocative and accompanied by thoughtful evaluations. The methods used can be widely applied in other arts and community development projects. They are a great resource for the field.

This fascinating book will be worth reading by community arts practitioners and environmental education staff in years to come.

Ailda Gersie, London-based dramatherapist and organisational consultant. Former Principal Lecturer in the Postgraduate Arts Therapies Department of the University of Hertfordshire, she has authored and edited several books.

We had no idea what to expect. My son and I. We had not had a chance to be alone together like this for some time. As we pitched camp and readied ourselves for the evening I remember feeling a little shy. Despite my usual confidence, I was starting to wonder if we had done the right thing coming here. We didn't know anyone. We were all here because we had one thing in common. Someone in our family was mixed race. Mixed race. What WAS that? What did it mean? Mixed up? Mixed together? Black? Brown? White? We were people. Not mixed. As we shared our evening meal with our fellow campers, all trepidation or nervousness disappeared. We were welcome for who we were. Not what we represented to society. Mixed race? Mixed feelings? No - we were us. A group of people with a common purpose. To have a fantastic weekend and to make new friends. To explore what makes us who we are and how we relate to each other? Yes - but not in an obvious way. And that's what made the camp unique. It was one of the happiest weekends of my life and my son's.

Katie Grant. Parent and Poet.

Dedicated to the children who came on the river exe-pedition:

Alice, Anaya, Asha, Cyrus, Dulcie,
Ellen, Emily, Esmee, Femi, Isaac,
Isobel, Josh, Lily, Matteo, Maxwell, Maya,
Olivia B, Olivia M, Poppy, Sam, Somin,
Tommy, Yjumye, Zach.

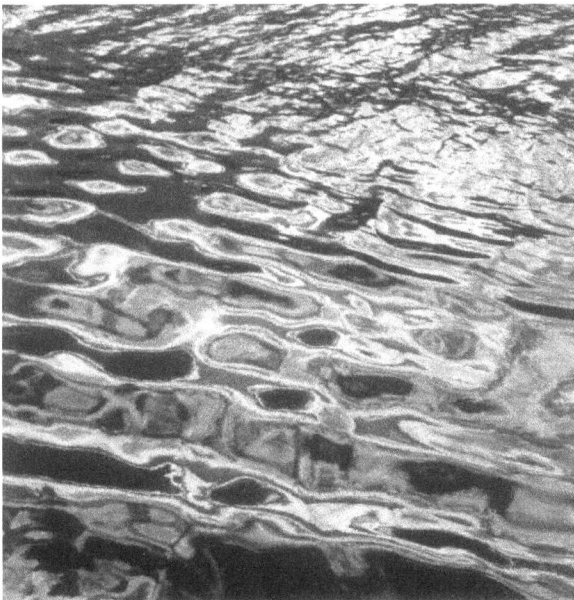

Insider Art (Publishing) Ltd.

PO Box 272. Exeter. EX2 9ZL

www.insiderart.org.uk

ISBN 978-0-9553400-5-5

Set in Tahoma 10pt

Blazing Tales
the river exe-pedition

A combined arts project with
mixed-heritage families in Devon

Sara Hurley

Edited by Karen Huckvale & Malcolm Learmonth

INSIDER ART

Publications from Insider Art

Love, Desire and Teen Spirit: Reflections on the Dynamic Force of Adolescent Eros by Joolz McLay 2009

ISBN: 978-0-9553400-2-4

A Jungian Circumambulation of Art & Therapy: Ornithology for the Birds by Michael Edwards 2010

ISBN: 978-0-9553400-3-1

The Untamed Sea: Paintings by Ronald Q. Henriques 2012

ISBN:978-0-9553400-4-8

Blazing Tales, 'the river exe-pedition': A combined arts project with mixed-heritage families in Devon by Sara Hurley 2013

ISBN:978-0-9553400-5-5

Blazing Tales, 'the river exe-pedition' Art Book by Sara Hurley 2014.

ISBN: 978-0-9553400-6-2

All books are available direct from the publisher: www.insiderart.org.uk postage free to UK addresses. Or can be ordered through bookshops.

Most books are also available worldwide direct from www.lulu.com (the printers) and online retailers.

Contents

Foreword: a personal introduction

Malcolm Learmonth

Not all those who wander are lost [1].

This Foreword is dedicated to Dr Chris Williams, who would regularly get a call in the small hours and drive the three and a half hours from Devon to Heathrow International airport, and help a person tortured in one world be believed and given sanctuary in another.

Chris particularly supported publishing this work, one of the roots of which was an evaluation prepared for the Self Heal Association, of which he was a Trustee.

'The river exe-pedition' is a handbook, a story and education about belonging, and the arts as educators of the heart.

The project itself, this book and the accompanying book of images, have been a labour of commitment and love it has been a privilege to be alongside.

It is a thought-provoking book being both pragmatic and about much more than it seems on first glance. It is an action-provoking book: good informed arts practice helping people live better together in a complex world. Sara's account combines thorough thinking, sensitive practice with straight-forward and clearly presented evaluation. And Sara gives sound advice for planning arts projects in rural places - notice where the bullocks drink from the river and try to avoid it - and practice - keep calm if bullocks arrive unexpectedly and want to join in...

All this the reader will find for themselves. My purpose is to offer some reflection on the books wider implications. We respond to images and stories largely through their resonance or contrast with our own experience: the more people who respond naturally through memory and imagination, the more effective the work. 'The river exe-pedition' had many resonances for me, some of them initially puzzling and hard to hear. My hope is that exploring why I, a white, middle aged, professional and apparently English man, was so carried away by 'the river exe-pedition' may encourage the readers own thoughts and feelings about what 'mixed heritage' might mean, and what the arts may bring to it.

In her introduction Sara makes a splendid rationale for the project itself and its evaluation. It makes sense:

- A local landscape overlies 'layers of global history', seen or unseen.
- Stories, histories and arts that people unfold from the landscape 'depended on individuals sense of belonging.'
- Sense of identity develops out of our interactions with the families, communities, places and landscape that tell us who we are, and where we are.
- In rural contexts, people with more than one cultural wellspring can experience the greater apparent homogeneity as making diverse cultural needs harder to meet that in the more overt melting pots of the cities.
- The projects' central question was 'How are these cultural needs met, and how can the arts support them?'
- The arts help us to think and feel obliquely: the project was 'steeped in metaphor.'
- To move within and between cultures we need to learn what does and does not 'carry over', (the literal meaning of metaphor), what translates and what does not. 'Metaphor', delightfully, is itself a metaphor: what do we "carry over"? What do we leave behind?
- Every family, every cultural combination generates unique experiences linked with identifiable threads: 'being in a mixed-heritage' family adds an extra dimension to parenting and identity issues; it's evident that basic issues are similar in most families.'
- Naming this complex area has produced 'no settled collective name': mixed race, mixed, dual heritage, multi heritage, bi-racial are all being used.
- The project asked: how are long-term senses of identity, acceptance and belonging negotiated when a child is one of very few like themselves?
- Paradoxically, the 'nature of the situation (means) it was not appropriate to constantly headline the issue'. Approaching such

sensitive areas of selfhood and relationship clumsily can easily itself become a declaration of someone's otherness.

- The arts, the metaphor bearers, are a natural mode of investigation and discovery, when more 'objective' methods may inadvertently do just that: objectify people, processes and complexity into categorisations.

But why did this apparently gentle journey of exploration down a Devon river move me personally?

As Sara noticed, common threads emerge from formative experiences of moving between cultural worlds. Perhaps there are many ways of 'growing up between worlds', of having mixed heritages. Can the experiences of people where the 'worlds' are relatively visible, like ethnicity, shed light on less visible experiences of childhoods in transit?

My own 'heritage' is not ethnically 'mixed': both my parents were Scots diaspora, I was born in India and brought up between England, Australia and Wales by non-English parents. I look English and now sound English. My cultural experiences between the ages of three and eleven, perhaps the age when acculturation is most imprinted, have made me, a 'Hidden Immigrant' in England. 'Hidden immigrants' will be presumed to understand cultural rules: in fact many aspects of 'Englishness' still baffle me.

I have borrowed the terms 'growing up among worlds', and 'hidden immigrant' from David Pollock and Ruth Van Reken. I found my resonance with 'the river exe-pedition' through their book, Third Culture Kids: Growing Up Among Worlds (1999)[2].

They use the term 'Third Culture Kid' (TCK), which emerged from work with (American) families whose children had grown up with extensive experience of other peoples, cultures and places.

Ethnicity was not the issue, cultural differences and not knowing how to answer the question 'Where are you from?' were. If my own story as an adult 'TCK' was one of the personal resonances with mixed heritage and the importance of story, making and landscape, then could the same thing illuminate other experiences of growing up between worlds?

Here are just a few more possible cultural 'worlds' people may grow up among more or less invisibly:

- Growing up in a family which has drastically changed class, (in either direction), in recent generations.
- Growing up in a foster family or 'in care'.
- Being the first, or last, in your family to go to university.
- Being sent away to boarding school.
- Sounding "posh" and working as a labourer with labourers.
- Working hard to lose your West Country accent for fear of being seen as a "yokel".
- Having or developing an impairment or disability.
- Going from being a Believer, (in anything, strongly enough), amongst Believers to becoming an Unbeliever.
- Having a sexual orientation or identity unacceptable in your social surroundings.
- Ageing: the past is a different country.
- Returning from war.
- Being a refugee.

'Culture' has been well defined as 'How We Do Things Round Here.' Every family and every primary school has a culture, every person who remembers the transition between knows something of being an "Adult Cross Cultural Kid".

The cultural worlds above are mostly social, class, wealth and power related. If family is in some ways a microcosm and the most influential culture of all, then can we describe the psychological landscapes and journeys among these 'home' worlds with a similar language? Consider the stories of crossings implicit for:

- A boy whose sole desire is to be a ballet dancer growing up in a military family.
- A girl whose whole family are highly extraverted, whilst she is innately introverted.
- The child who is the carer of a mentally ill parent, overtly or covertly.
- The under-stimulated yet gifted child at home and school.
- Being a twin.

- Being the adopted child.
- Being the sibling with a different father.

Who am I? Who are we? Where do I belong? These are the soul-searching questions common to those who have grown up among worlds. That is why this book may have something to say to all of us about the riches, the losses of transition and the common ambivalence of our sense of self, place and community.

Like Sara, the TCK researchers identify threads of common experience. The 'costs' often include:

- Rootlessness and restlessness.
- Unresolved grief.
- Shaming experiences of cultural ignorance.

Each arises from a struggle to accommodate likeness and difference. Identity issues are more problematic when likeness and differences are apparently conflicted, and have to be balanced. Pollock and Van Reken identify these ways of coping in different cultural worlds:

Foreigner: Look different / think different	Hidden immigrant Look alike / think different
Adopted Look different / think alike	Mirror: Look alike / think alike

Some strategies for negotiating are:

- **Chameleons**: emphasise likeness over difference, (I'm just like you).
- **Screamers**: emphasise difference over likeness (I'm not like you, even if I look like you, and I don't want to be).
- **Wallflowers**: rather than risk exposure as different stand back, hope to be unseen, and take notes for as long as possible.

Attachment Theory developed by John Bowlby (Holmes. 1993)[3] demonstrates that developmentally we learn who we are through concentric circles of mirroring: our lovability, acceptability, agency, and value are all learnt by seeing our reflections in the eyes of others.

If the world's mirrors keep changing the reflections that inform our development can be richer, more tolerant and complex understandings of ourselves, others and the world. The curse can be a homelessness where we are only at home with the equally homeless.

Transitions entail losses. The literal TCK gets on a plane on one side of the world and gets out on the other having left important parts of their status, lifestyle, possessions, relationships, role models, and pasts behind. The reflections have changed, so the experience of self becomes discontinuous, and the social world unpredictable.

The grief is real, and so, frequently, is the shame endured about not knowing 'How We Do Things Around Here'. Imagine being brought up to be good by never, ever flushing a toilet unnecessarily because water is scarce and precious, and then being 'good' in Basildon.

The experience of growing up among worlds which are parallel and transited less visibly daily, weekly or termly is mostly less dramatic. Though this can have its moments: remembering slipping between 'school' and 'home' worlds by absent-mindedly calling my teacher 'Mum' at the age of six can still make me wince.

Shaming experiences are often the teacher of what we must declare, surrender, smuggle secretly, or carry as a gift across a cultural border.

I remember with deep warmth and gratitude the man who taught me a little of how kindness, intelligence and an understanding the arts could help a very visible immigrant.

As a six year old I was in the only English-speaking class of a Welsh language primary school.

As an eight year old I had been physically dragged to the back of an Australian class with two other boys to be caned. I escaped the actual assault, on that occasion, but watched, terrified, as the teacher broke his cane in two on the hand of the boy in front of me. The past is a world too, and in that world this was not abnormal.

As a nine-year-old I was in the "Special" class at an Australian primary school. It didn't occur to me to ask whether that was because I was especially bright or especially disruptive. Knowing or thinking too much was a ostracisable offence amongst my peers, so it may well have been both.

One day the Special Class teacher, Mr Scardoni, brought a new song for us to learn, a translation of the traditional Welsh folk song 'Jenny Jones'. I have only just realized that he probably did this for me. The song began

Light-hearted I stroll through the Vale of Llangollen

I never spoke Welsh, but I knew how it sounded, how the letters made the right sounds, and that it was different from English. The 'double l' sound is made by shaping an L in your mouth and gently blowing. It definitely wasn't said 'Langolen'. I had to say so.

This 'screamer' tendency to come over as a 'know all' was a bad mixture with the prevailing belief in the unmanliness of intelligence and frequently got me into fights. I remember one that started with the taunt 'You swallowed an encyclopaedia have you?' My parents really were writing an encyclopaedia at the time, so I probably hit him first.

I had also tried to answer 'Where are you from?' with 'Earth. And you?' This started fights in Australia and stopped conversations dead in England, as I secretly wanted it to. One way of controlling loss is to get your rejection in first, and keep as much self-esteem as possible: 'I wouldn't be like you if you paid me.'

So it was with a feeling of 'here we go again' that I said I had been to Llangollen, and demonstrated how to say it properly. Mr Scardoni said he really hadn't known that, it was terribly interesting, and he thought everybody should learn this interesting new thing, if I could teach the class to make the right sound, (and he knew how all the boys liked new and rather rude sounding noises), then we could sing the song properly. We did.

This inspired intervention, (genius for an Australian school in 1967), spoke directly to the heart of my rage and alienation. Difference was valued. Knowledge was valid.

We stayed in the 'Special' class for two years: the continuity itself was a blessing. The following year I painted what I knew was my first real painting: a curving twilit river: on the bank just one slender autumn tree.

I think now the painting was saturated with loss and longing, a soul homesickness partly geographical, partly temporal, partly cultural, partly nostalgia for a world that never was, and partly the dimming of childhood vision. It is the melancholy but almost enjoyable and insatiable longing that in Welsh is called *hwraeth*. The painting was equally saturated with the joy of remembered beauty, its aliveness in imagination and the discovery of a door into an inner landscape. In a way it foreshadowed every authentic piece of art I have made since. Mr Scardoni framed the painting and hung it in the corridor outside our classroom.

Mr Scardoni was an immigrant himself. I believe he created these turning points out of his experience, using language, validation and song to make a bridge between worlds. Singing brings human beings alongside one another: it literally attunes us. To help teach a song was to be profoundly included. 'Teach us one of your songs' is a moment that can easily be imagined when a group embraced a stranger 60,000 years ago.

Mr Scardoni honoured the essential loneliness of the painting, fanned some ability and, perhaps most importantly, intentionally or unintentionally, showed me that art-making itself was a survival strategy. (I'd already learnt that drawing Spitfires best was a very tradable commodity in the peer respect stakes). Somehow the arts seemed to help the boundaries between the worlds to become more permeable, and definitions of inclusion and otherness to soften a little.

Mr Scardoni and Blazing Tales both understood how the questions: who am I? where am I from? where do I belong? are deepened for movers between worlds, and they intuited that the arts could contain the costs whilst increasing the benefits of the experience.

Here were some of my resonances with 'the river exe-peditions' deep understanding of the importance of arts as agents of exploration, validation and valuation and why oblique strategies are best when trying to bridge worlds. Blazing Tales had skilfully cooked into this project some of the very medicines that had helped me.

We need to be ourselves, seen and validated as such, and to be a part of a group. Cultures emphasize the 'right' point on the spectrum between 'me' and 'us' very differently. The Japanese research on TCK's is entirely concerned with the social impact of returnees on the home culture. Western research is almost entirely on the impact on the individual.

Cultures differ as much in arts practice as they do beliefs about human nature. But somehow the arts can also help open the gates to being alongside. On the cultural level of permeability here is just one example of the arts joyously weed-like ability to leap fences:

'The Miller's Wedding', a traditional Strathspey dance tune was being played in Scotland before 1788. The same tune can now be heard as:

- A Japanese song, 'Glow of a Firefly', describing the hardships of poor scholars and used at closing time in restaurants.
- A Dutch football song, 'We Love Orange.'
- A Thai song, 'Together in Unity', sung after sports events and believed to be a Thai traditional tune.

It was also Korea's national anthem. Everybody, it seems, likes a good tune and found one in 'Auld Lang Syne', which is also 'The Miller's Wedding' but slowed and given words in Scots English, or 'Lallans', (incomprehensible to most English speakers), by Robert Burns less than 250 years ago.

This is not an isolated example: if the blues originated anywhere it was Mali. The word 'guitar', and presumably ancestors of the instrument, were passed from Persian to ancient Greek, to Latin, to Arabic to Spanish to English. The continuity of cultural permeability through the arts has been underestimated.

The arts can be equally powerful definitions of difference: from initiatory scars to anthems, uniforms, and flags they can make for greater impermeability. Years ago in Northern Ireland I was told that the friendly questions about musical tastes were 'diagnostic' of loyalties thus 'do you like Irish music?' was a proxy sectarian enquiry. The arts were encoded descriptors of difference and defences against otherness.

In the film 'Casablanca' when the denizens of Rick's Bar drown out the Nazis singing 'The Watch on the Rhine': *Repay our shame with our foes blood!* with 'La Marseillaise': *Let impure blood water our furrows!* the 'Us' and 'Them' seem strangely similar. Even arts pressed into the service of impermeability tend to escape and misbehave. The tune of 'The Watch on the Rhine' was also used for Harvard's alumni song 'Bright College Years'.

The arts can serve permeability spontaneously like weeds, but can also deliberately cultivate it. Peace Choirs sang the songs everyone knew across the barbed wire in divided Cyprus.

The arts help to define who is "we", and who is not, as groups within cultures too. Growing up, it was good to know that 'our' music was 'their' noise.

This double capacity of art to loosen and tighten how we construe thoughts, feelings, narratives, group and identity, is key to how my work as an art psychotherapist helps people to negotiate transitions. Something similar seems to happen with cultures: anthropologists note that cultural stress leads to more art-making. What is the mechanism for this connection?

The arts cluster around transitions because they resource us for them. Immersion in the arts implies a movement among worlds, the movement carries us on tides that ebb and flow between:

- Inner and Outer
- Self and Other
- Thinking and Feeling
- Uniqueness and Commonality
- Discipline and Spontaneity
- Control and Accident
- Validation and Invisibility
- Safety and Anxiety
- Transparency and Secrecy

This mercurial quality of natural movement between in the arts seems to offer a parallel with the psychological emotional and social demands of being among worlds.

To participate in making and sharing art alongside others permits us to be both seen *and* heard, rather than *not* seen *or* heard. When our gaze is shared in the work, we can meet without confrontation. To sing together we need to hear that sameness of the tune not the difference of the singers.

Mr Scardoni and Blazing Tales did a kind of alchemy. Alchemy begins with a well-wrought vessel that can contain without constraining, and hold without defining, the ambivalence and the complexity of movements between worlds.

This is skilled work: the potential for humiliation is never very far away. Yet if it is successful it can transmute the conflicts of those who have grown up among worlds into complex understandings by embracing them. The arts are at home with paradox: the benefits outweigh the costs of growing up among worlds if we can experience difference as related by *and* rather than *or*. My experience is unique and I can be recognised in a group for instance.

'Third culture' is the evolution of a perspective that sees the relativity of worlds and redefines conflict as complexity.

'The river exe-pedition' project directly addressed another of these areas of ambivalence: Sense of Place.

I once stood on a Welsh hilltop with a man who could tell me who had owned every field we could see for generations. I once read of a blind man, who had committed the view from Brent Knoll in Somerset to his mind's eye before he lost his sight, and could still climb his hill and see it. These men were orientated. Landscapes too, hold a mirror to who we are, and their loss can be literally dis-orientating.

As a child the longing for the lost landscape re imagined in my painting felt like a physical ache. At the same time seeing aboriginal shell middens, less than 150 years old, in Tasmania felt like direct contact with the only completely successful genocide that we know of. I felt these people had known, and in some way been known by, the Tasmanian land in a way I never could be. It was stolen land, and I was ashamed. I had been educated outside school on the subject. Most memorably by my mother who - when I sang a song at home with the chorus *Oh how I wish that I could be, a happy little aborigine!* - explained exactly why I didn't.

The conflict felt overt, present, and raw in these landscapes, yet invisible in white Australia. Although the government actually ran a 'White Australia' immigration policy and called it that. It made for an uneasy relationship with a beautiful landscape that felt like it could shrug us off its shoulders in a second, and may yet.

Mostly though the world has been smaller, more complicated, more permeable, connected and surprising than we think. Continuity and disruption run through the same landscape. In the Devon landscape around 'the river exe-pedition' there are threads of continuity in the world:

- One of the oldest so far known proofs of modern humans in northern Europe was found in a cave in Torquay.

- When a very ancient bone from Wookey Hole Caves in Somerset had a good enough DNA to look for descendants a direct matrilineal match was found teaching history in a local school.

- Many hedges in Devon are a thousand years old and more.

- The Heavitree Yew in Exeter is almost certainly older than the 12th Century church it stands beside.

- There has been a Jewish presence in Exeter, (apart from when banished), since at least 1161: the current synagogue dates from 1764.

There are threads of connection between worlds:

- There was trade between the South West and the Mediterranean by 600 BCE.

- Devon dialect can be heard almost unaltered among fishermen in Newfoundland.

- In the Second World War the air defence of Exeter was largely flown by Polish pilots.

There are threads of competing worlds:

- Exeter was occupied by Anglo Saxons in 658, and the city had a Welsh speaking 'British Quarter' until 928. Nearly 1100 years later the name for Exeter, Caerwysc, is still remembered in the Welsh language. The name of the river has scarcely changed: it is Celtic and means The Water.

- Until the 16th century there was a slave trade between Southwest England and North Africa, with Africans as the slavers.

- Barbary corsairs - pirates - regularly raided coastal villages and kidnapped hundreds. At one place in Cornwall you can see what are claimed to be their cannonballs.

- In the 19th century a Bristol Slaver went down on a North Devon beach and African bones are still sometimes found.

Cultural worlds have always fought, traded, married and swapped songs. We happen to know about the Somerset history teacher's mothers, yet ancestral DNA has a delightful tendency to confound bigotry. A righteous advocate for Native American Indian rights made the mistake of conducting a similar DNA experiment in public and found out that he simply wasn't what he thought he was.

Devon's is a deeply maternal landscape. If you dig a bit of earth long enough it centres you. For potters it is only the spinning clay (earth) being centred on the wheel which allows them to 'pull' the vessel into an inside and an outside. It means leaning into, and trusting. One of the most effective kindnesses for refugees from torture in another world is to give them an allotment. Some things will grow the same as at home, others are new, and delicious if you acquire the taste. My own journey, over and over has led me back to the land and landscape for orientation. Befriending a landscape is as close to being home as I know.

Hidden diversity is common, in people, in families, in cultures and between cultures. Human geography's rivers of class, gender, history, war, oppression, religion, education sculpt less visible landscapes as surely as Exe has her valley.

The more layers superimposed on our maps of inner and outer geographies, the greater will be both our potential confusion and our potential to manage complexity.

The terrors of cultural impermeability are equally real:

- African / Caribbean people in the UK are between 2 and 8 times more likely to be diagnosed with schizophrenia.

- Black and mixed race people are 2 to 3 times more likely than the general population to be admitted to psychiatric hospital.

- Black men, with no evidence whatsoever that they are more violent than another group, are perceived once hospitalised as more dangerous than white men.

Perhaps living between cultures with oppression, invalidation and inequality built in drives people mad, or difference is being defined as mad and bad, or both.

Eating and drinking what you literally believe to be Christ's flesh and blood on Sundays makes you a Catholic. In another context compulsive symbolic cannibalism might seem diagnosable as a mental health problem.

We simply do not know until we ask - and spend a lot of time listening - what layers of cultural mapping, memory and trauma, adaptation and denial make sense in another person's world, or how they may understand ours. When we act from incompatible assumptions, it has been wisely said that the only objective measure of insanity is what the people around you will not put up with.

Diversity is often hidden because we don't see what we don't see, especially about ourselves. A Geordie hitch-hiking in the U.S. is supposed to have been kindly picked up by a Texan truck driver who asked him, *'What the haell is that accent y'all got thaya?'* The Geordie explained he was from the north of England. The truck driver shook his head and replied sympathetically *'Gee, Ah'm sure as haell glad I ain't got no accent'.*

Who am I? Who are we? Where do I belong?

If we have to guess the answers reflected in a world that keeps flickering, experience of self and other will keep flickering too. But that in itself makes for a world view which knows that presumptions seeming very solid, presumed, immutable and innate are in fact local and transitory. It is also exactly what makes world-shifters 'the prototype Citizens of the future', whatever those worlds have been.

The gift for the cultures not threatened by the evolution of third cultures is to see themselves. Perhaps only a mature and sophisticated 'Adult Cross Culture Kid' could have told the United States this to its face, and been in a position to do so:

We live in a culture that discourages empathy. A culture that too often tells us our principal goal in life is to be rich, thin, young, famous, safe, and entertained. (Obama, 2007)[4]

No wonder they asked 'where are you from?', and wanted to see his birth certificate.

'The river exe-pedition' brought awareness of being on a planet to a focus in some Devon fields, telling us important things about being a human being anywhere, and showing skilled use of the arts. It was a gift to its participants. It was also learning with and from them, and that is their gift to this book. It is delight to see that learning presented here so lucidly and convincingly, without losing any of its poetry. It is an incentive to all of us to embrace our own joyous mongrel-ness.

Liminality (*liminus:* threshold) is the state of in-between-ness, or of being on both sides of a border. It is also used to describe the space between the tides on a shoreline. Many of us have picked up pebbles, sea varnished and shining from the shore and carried home what we believed was a gem, only to see it turn back into a pebble. There is a special quality that only breathes in the spaces between. The gem can remain a gem through the arts.

What of the River itself? Rivers run through our lives in every way: befriending the landscape is a gift to those between worlds. And the rivers shape those landscapes. The choice of the River Exe as a theme for finding and exploring a sense of place and story in this landscape was a good one, because the Exe is a silver thread that led to a story. All rivers slip easily into being The River: The River that resonates the shape of lives from sparkling rushing joie de vivre to power that can flood a city. To the estuary where with each tide the river calmly loses its identity in the sea, yet can still be smelt and traced by a returning salmon from a thousand miles away. The River is circular: ocean water falls as rain on Exmoor, and the Exe is how it returns.

The River itself is defined by a journey from the oceanic and unified, through a specific identity and back. There is something of this rhythm to the journeys of those between worlds. Between different rivers that tell the different, but similar, stories about being human and being human in the context of a particular place, time and culture. Having the experience of this movement more than once can bring a heightened sense of both what is specific and unique, and what is deeply shared, and value both. Nurturing the voyagers between cultural worlds brings gifts a healthy culture will see as essential to understanding itself, to mutual enrichment, to growth in a human, rather than an economic sense. The River of this book is a pragmatic, deeply thought and felt contribution to how we can help that happen.

You may need to take your shoes and socks off.

Malcolm Learmonth.

Exeter 2013

Series Introduction

This is the fourth publication from Insider Art for general distribution.

It is the nature of both art and psychotherapy to be 'liminal': to be 'boundary dwelling'. Both imply journeys between inner and outer, rigour and spontaneity, past, present and future, relationship and identity. Combining liminalities, inevitably amplifies them. This holds true beyond arts and psychotherapy extending to projects invoking the arts as agents of change in health and social contexts, as the aims and methods are broadly, if not overtly, psychological.

Insider Art's interest in publication began with the realisation that 'professional' literatures are bound to focus on discrete and defined areas, emphasising categories and difference over interconnection and resonance. Arts literature tends towards the self-referential, vague, un-evidenced and fashion based. Neither mode is terribly interested in what kind of eco-system they might co-inhabit. It is a little like a rope maker and a knot specialist not noticing they were looking at a net.

The books we have so far edited and published have looked at: depth psychology, art history and the antecedents of art therapy (Edwards); the inevitable presence of desire and eros in therapy (McClay); the extraordinary paintings of a man neither an 'In' or 'Out' sider artist (Henriques) and the current volume. Our aim is to make nets knotted from the disciplined thinking of professional writing and the 'how long is a piece of string' open-ness and subjectivity of creative processes.

The search for what connects, as well as for what differentiates, will often not meet conventional publication criteria, yet frequently characterises some of the most interesting and eloquent work we see.

Collectively we are losing faith in 'evidence' that atomises lived experience by extorting the numbers demanded by a tyrannical, ludicrous premise that profit is the ultimate human good, end and means. Empathy, community, resilience, reflection, knowledge, questioning, creativity, the price of the countable and the value of the uncountable are as important to human beings -if not more so- than greed and competition.

Malcolm Learmonth & Karen Huckvale. Series Editors.

Acknowledgements

I'd like to wholeheartedly thank everyone who has helped make these two books possible. To the families who adventured with us; to Hugh Nankivell and Cara Roxanne for their inspiring work, facilitation and embracing of the project; to Tony Walker who documented our journey in film; Parminder Southcott and Kayte Price for opening the door to Blazing Tales and to Lu Christie for her creative input on the Tail to Tale project 2007. To Chukumeka Maxwell for his encouragement; Lucy MacKeith for her support and guidance about black history in Devon, Phil Smith 'The Crab Man' for his mis-guided tour. To Carrie Domingos who provided administrative support and Jeremy Holloway our lead volunteer. Thanks also go to Hannah Reeves at the Spacex Contemporary Art Gallery, Exeter; Philippa Wood from the Royal Albert Memorial Museum and St Nicholas Priory, Exeter; The Croal Family of Exmouth and Stuart Line Cruises, Exmouth.

Special mention and thanks go to my children, Josh, Yjumye and Femi for their encouragement behind the scenes and being my best teachers. Huge thanks to the editors, Karen Huckvale and Malcolm Learmonth for their tireless patience and enthusiastic support of this work; and for being both finicky and fabulous at the same time. Thanks also to Sarah Holmes of Insider Art for the graphs and charts. Finally, thanks to the funders for recognising the value of this project and making the whole thing possible: The National Lottery and The Self Heal Association.

LOTTERY FUNDED   SELF HEAL ASSOCIATION

Sara Hurley
Exeter 2013

Part One
About the book, Blazing Tales and the author

Blazing Tales' hope this book provides inspiration for individuals and organisations who work with groups to explore their local spaces and places, whilst giving practical information for going about such a project. It brings attention to the relationship that different members of a mixed-heritage family have with the British countryside. In difficult times of social and environmental change alongside physical and emotional dislocation we think this is important work that has particular resonance for mixed-heritage families living in rural Britain.

The arts, and arts practitioners, often possess the type of skills and knowledge that serve as a bridge to connect people with places and each other. This book tells the story of a combined arts project for rurally based, mixed-heritage families called 'the river exe-pedition'. Led by creative arts company 'Blazing Tales' in 2009, the project took its name from the River Exe, in south-west England, along whose route a total of fifteen families attended three day workshops and two weekend camps.

There are many stories and voices inside these pages. From the thought provoking foreword by editor, Malcolm Learmonth to the voices of family members, as well as each artist talking from the perspective of their own art forms.

The accompanying 'art book' shows some of the art, songs, stories and poems made on the project. This book tells and the other book shows. They are a pair and make sense of each other, therefore reading them together is helpful. The books have come out of a specific project and offer general, practical insights into setting up and leading workshops, as well as sharing ideas for combined arts activities in the environment.

The story of the families' creative journey along the river is told through the detail of the workshops that happened in each place. The project evaluation is in an appendix at the back of the book: showing the questions that the project was addressing, giving voice to the participants and charting the natural progression of events.

There are thousands of life-changing, life-enhancing creative arts and community projects happening all over Britain at any one time. Each with the potential to make a distinct difference to people's lives. Here was another one - so why have we bothered to write a book about it? The book started life as a report for Exeter charity The Self-Heal Association.

The charity considered its themes and insights worth sharing with a wider audience. With the invaluable support of Insider Art this book and its sister have now been published.

Blazing Tales

Blazing Tales is a combined arts company that bring stories to life using visual art, music, story work and digital media. Working with communities, specific places and landscapes we draw inspiration from its stories to create new art, performance or exhibitions with people. We are a group of participatory artists and performers who enable people to express themselves creatively and find form for their voices to be heard. We aim to make high quality art work and bring out the best in people, whilst seeking to develop skills, confidence, creativity and improved well-being for the people we work with.

We like to work outside and wherever possible lead projects in the environment. Designing combined arts workshops that help people to connect with their immediate environment and its stories. We believe that supporting a sense of belonging can be of positive benefit to individuals, the people around them and the places they go. The company has a special interest in working with rurally based mixed-heritage families and has led several projects with this group.

About the author

Sara Hurley is a storyteller, actor, writer and participatory artist. She leads workshops in storytelling, story making, drama and creative literacy and performs as a teller of traditional tales. Her story work also involves creatively working with real life, personal stories. She lives in Devon, where she grew up, and enjoys the outdoor life. A keen and intrepid traveller her work has taken her to India and Africa. She is artistic director of 'Blazing Tales'.

Sara's Story

I came to live in Devon when I was 12 after a move from Bedford; from the River Ouse to the River Exe. Changing schools from an open plan, new build in a multi-cultural town to the last year of a traditional grammar school in a Devon market town where teachers wore mortar boards and I learnt Latin. Noticing the differences at that time probably had a long lasting effect on me.

I came to love and appreciate the south-west corner of England. Its rural heritage struck a chord with my own long, family history in the hills of Somerset and Gloucestershire. As a young person I would often look outwards - over the seas, imagining life in faraway places. Usually hot countries whose colour and music made me want to dance my socks off or to the story lands of my companionable fairy tale book.

As an adult I've been lucky enough to dance with the dust between my toes in the southern hemisphere on many occasions. The beat of the drum took me deep into another culture showing and teaching me things I otherwise would never have known or understood from the inside. I have a son who is half Devonian and two daughters who are half Sierra Leonian. In fact my girls could be called Sierra-Devonian!

I can never know what my daughter's experience of being mixed really is, that's for them to understand. This work began with me trying to make sense of my own story - of having a home experience hardly shared with anyone else living around me despite being an active member of my community. Of having a rooted, in the bones, sense of my rustic, English heritage whilst having been changed through direct experience of another culture I empathised with and came to know well. If it was like that for me then what was it like for my children and other families?

Living in a mixed family in a small, rural town and being a storyteller, educator and participatory artist led me to explore this work in this way. Around this time I set up Blazing Tales and met a local organisation that brought mixed-heritage families together called The Planet Rainbow Project. Our first project was with this group and the river project came out of that relationship.

I continue to work creatively with stories in the environment as much as I can, in education, health or community work. Underpinning enjoyment and learning experiences with environmental, historical and cultural awareness of wherever I am – ready to look at exactly what I'm seeing as well as what has been hidden out of sight.

Velvet Dresses
Louisa Adjoa Parker

Louisa Adjoa Parker is a West Country poet, who writes about her experiences as a mixed heritage woman. She is the daughter of a British mother and Ghanaian father, and was born in the UK. She has lived most of her life in the South West of England. Her collection *Salt-sweat and Tears* was published by Cinnamon Press in 2007[1]. The poem Velvet Dresses is from that collection and she has kindly given permission for this poem to be included here. The poem talks about Dorset, a neighbouring county to Devon in the West Country.

Velvet Dresses

I want to climb under Dorset's skin
Curl up in her folds, wrap her around me
Like a patchwork quilt, stained
Yet stitched with years of love,
Taste the colours of green and gold,
Run my fingers over rough textures
Of ancient earth

I want to crawl under her pavements,
Her roads; lift great slabs of Tarmac,
Climb every craggy, awkward hill
Every cliff like a tooth capped with gold;
trek for miles through woods
and green fields like velvet dresses
with skirts fanned out wide;

I want to sink my fingers into the earth,
Let the tiny stones and grit and bones
Run through my hand;
Search for the past along with
Fossils spiralling to dust
In clay-rich soil.

I want to let Dorset's past soak
Like cocoa butter into my skin,
Let it's history merge with mine:
Talk of Africa and her slaves.

I want to know it will be fine
For anyone with not from here etched
Like tribal markings into their skin,
To sink into Dorset like a warm rock-pool,
With fingers stretched out towards the sun;
To walk her beaches, green velvet fields
With pride, say,

I live here, I belong here, she is mine.

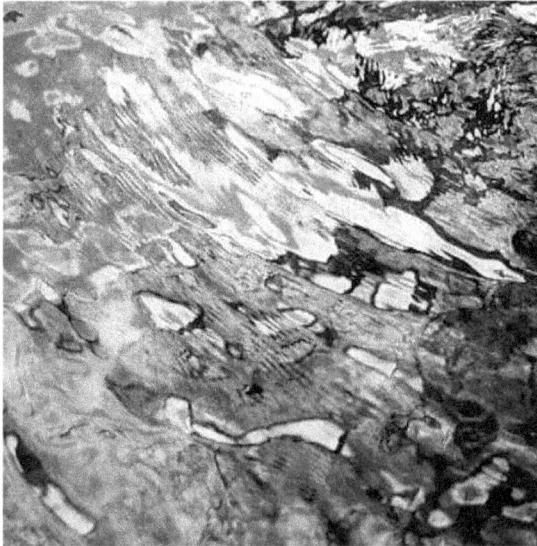

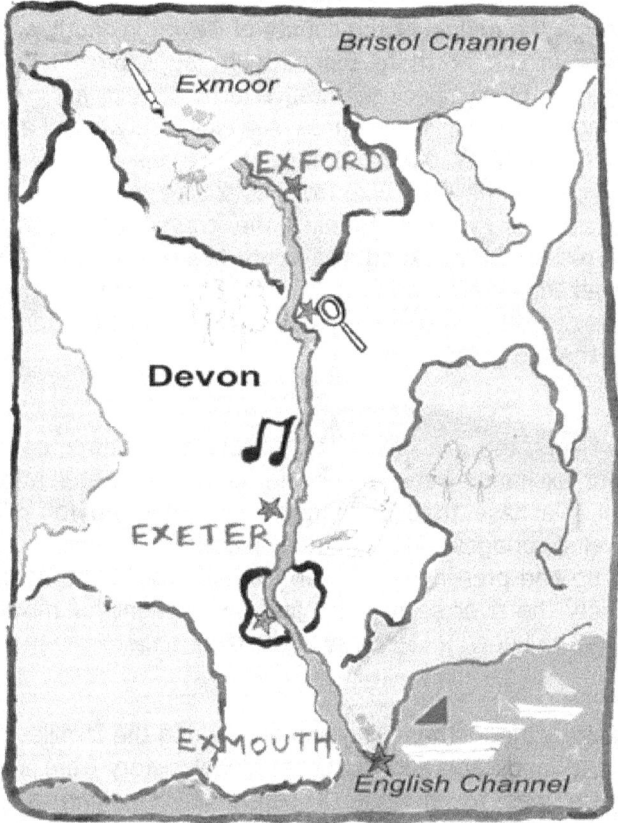

Map of Devon showing the route of the River Exe.
Stars mark the places we visited.

Introduction

The River Exe begins high on open moorland before dropping down through wooded river valleys, pastoral meanders and on to the city quay before reaching the open sea.

It runs through the middle of the county of Devon in south-west England from Exmoor in the north to Exmouth in the south. 'The river exe-pedition' was a place specific, creative arts project for rurally based mixed-heritage families. Over three seasons, between February and November, the families participated in workshops as they adventured along the banks of the River Exe from its source to the sea. Workshops were held at five locations running the course of the river. These included: a residential weekend at a youth hostel in Exford; a residential camping weekend on a farm in the Exe Valley; a day on the river bank on the outskirts of Exeter; a discovery day in central Exeter; and a boat trip and day by the sea in Exmouth.

As with all rivers, the Exe has a long history as a source of sustenance and point of exchange between people, creatures, water and land. On the Exe, people have tried to manage it's dynamism for millennia by building weirs, bridges and crossing places and more recently, by cleaning it up and preserving natural habitats around the estuary. In its infinite variety the river seemed an apt environment for mixed-heritage families to get to know. (Hurley in Schieffelin, Gersie & Nanson 2014)[1]

Through song-writing, storytelling and art making the families explored a changing local landscape and looked at global history from a local level. Our intention was to increase a sense of belonging and improve knowledge about where they live whilst introducing them to places they otherwise might not visit. Through the opportunity of being together relationships and networks were strengthened and family experiences shared.

The project asked questions about their relationship with where they live, why they came together and looked below the surface at the history and environment along the River Exe. The mixed population is known to be growing fast and little research has been published to date about the experience of mixed-heritage families or individuals who live in the rural regions of Britain. Whilst this book opens a window on the rural mixed-heritage experience, it is, after all, an account of an arts project. It shows how artists work to facilitate stronger connections between people, places and each other, whilst providing ways for people to express themselves and the means for their voices to be heard. Therefore, the book is intended to serve as a provocation for conversation and debate about the experience that may lead to further action on behalf of mixed-heritage people living in rural areas. More questions have come to light than have been answered and there are many issues to consider, particularly for mixed children and young people growing up. How their social and cultural needs are met and how can the arts support them?

The project was multi-layered. The following sections consider the layering involved.

Arts Workshops

The workshops and their locations were the main attraction for the families. Each event provided time out from normal life to spend with the family doing fun, new and interesting things that were suitable for all age groups. Developing skills and confidence to approach creativity as a means of expression was inextricably linked with the social aspect of the project. Engagement with creative process through music, visual art and stories was the primary focus for people. Families were 'doing' creative processes whilst 'being' together.

Whilst providing fun and meaningful experiences, the artistic side of the project also aimed to improve each participant's confidence to express themselves creatively. Ideas for accessible, outdoor, creative activities were shared that could be repeated afterwards when the families went out on their own. The participants got to know the facilitation style of the artists which supported them to try it for themselves in a similar way.

Participatory arts practice goes hand in hand with the idea that everybody has creative potential. It's not necessary to be a creative genius but it is necessary to make the conditions in which to be creative. A workshop provides the kind of time, space and guidance that helps the creative process along. It's a space where connections can be made within the themes and frameworks for expression that are offered. The kind of experiences that take place in a workshop support experiential learning and make memories that a person can translate into other experiences.

Is it enough to just be immersed in the process? What about artistic product? Having an end result, a product or performance, culminates a workshop well. Showing what can be achieved, surprising yourself, feeling proud or fulfilled and working as a group all contribute to improved well-being, whatever age you are. It is possible to make quality artistic products in a mixed group of participants and challenge the assumption that product doesn't matter. Balancing the creative process and making good enough art work is at the facilitator's discretion and each workshop has unique parameters.

Creativity is an intrinsic part of being human and human beings are complex. Finding personal creativity and being creative is rarely a straightforward process. Creative expression is deeply personal and can feel exposing at first; generally speaking it's a sensitive creature before it finds its feet. Often creativity is spoken about as a separate entity and it's worth remembering that each person's relationship to their creativity, including history of play and self-expression, is as individual as they are. During a workshop creative facilitators have a lot of responsibility to individual well-being beyond the accepted rules of care, and health and safety guidelines.

Designing and leading creative workshops for mixed-heritage families involved consideration of age, gender and cultural differences as well as a wide range of experience and familiarity with the creative process. Activities needed to be designed with these things in mind and to be open and welcoming to everyone. We aimed to encourage adult participation and discourage parent(s) and carers watching their children from the side-lines or being vicariously creative. What happened during the river workshops, in the conditions and parameters we provided, was that everything we made told a new story about the place and was a unique and fresh contribution made by the group.

Combined Arts

Arts that cross artistic and cultural boundaries and which share ideas and expertise across disciplines are continuing to grow.....many work at the point where art, culture and communities meet.

Arts Council England 2010[2]

Small-scale, combined arts companies, like Blazing Tales, are often found working at a local level, leading projects that engage directly with communities. A multi-disciplinary approach is well suited to working in outdoor environments and not-for-purpose venues. Many artists have cross-over skills and many art, performance and community projects are the outcome of this kind of cross-fertilization.

Artists working in this way bring expertise from the breadth of their own practise with a willingness to explore new, innovative ways of combining art forms. Working closely with other artists, picking up ideas and developing them from an alternative discipline extends the creative and social experience for artists and participants alike. The evident mutual understanding and team working by the artists models a co-operative approach which can positively benefit participants confidence in the facilitators and the project.

Different people have tendencies toward different styles of thinking and learning: visual, aural and kinaesthetic. (O'Connor & Seymour 1990)[3] Taking a combined arts approach accommodates and satisfies different learning styles, allowing all the participants to find activities which are both comfortable and challenging.

Clear leadership and programme structure provide recognisable boundaries alongside accessible, fun and innovative activities which encourage personal and creative exploration. This supports people to comfortably and safely express themselves.

For this project one artist led the main activity at each event while other artists took their inspiration from them. However, the workshops were all interlinked with each artist stepping up where necessary in response to participants or the vagaries of the workshop environment. On the river exe-pedition the workshops were cumulative and evolving, each one threading on from the last towards an end point.

Place

Playing, singing, telling stories and making art can help to strengthen the bonds between people and their connection to the specific place they are in. If that environment is the area in which they live, then making an informed relationship with it creates a lasting experience that can positively affect behaviour. Participants are more likely to feel an attachment to the place and therefore care more about it.

The Black Environment Network (BEN) exists to reach out to ethnic communities in order to stimulate participation....They believe that in the process people may be empowered through gaining essential skills in self-help, self-representation and self-improvement - the effects of which spread into areas of life far beyond environmental involvement. (BEN 2013)[4]

Through looking at the older stories of a place people can become more able to find new ways of expressing their own stories. Through getting to know a place people can make new memories and build a fresh relationship with it. Peoples relationship to what may have happened in a place before, in history or story, may impact on these stories or not. Either way the making of meaning in personal narratives, increasing a sense of belonging and of being part of a continuum is helped.

Where we were, who we were and the time of year were pertinent and fundamental to the choices we made about the workshop content. For example, starting the project on high ground in spring close to where the river begins completely affected everything we did and how a new group responded. Being at the sea-side in late autumn and gazing at distant horizons with a group who all know each other informed the creative response in new ways. Working site-specifically gives people a direct personal experience where nothing is lost in translation regardless of how old you are. An outside workshop is as unique as a live performance as it will only ever happen once exactly in that way. The sensory immediacy of the environment helps make a personal involvement with the place. When matched with participating in a memorable activity and knowledge building about the place then a vibrant, meaningful connection can potentially be made.

Devon is a large and rural county with a patch-work of villages, market towns and one city. The families were invited to visit locations within their county, often close to home, that they would not ordinarily go to or had never been to before. They came from varied circumstance, brought together through their experience of being mixed-heritage in a rural region. Families said they frequently felt isolated with their children often being in a tiny, mis-understood minority. Few families regularly accessed the surrounding countryside, explored new places or had much historical knowledge about the area they lived in.

Being in a mixed-heritage family is culturally complex. Our project sought to ask how can these children and families make, and maintain, a relationship with their environment when they have 'not from here etched on their skin'. (Parker. 2007)[5] Our families began with a compromised sense of belonging because their mixed-ness objectively placed them as outsiders. As Devon was home, and most of the children were born here, there was a need to build up their own unique relationship to where they live and claim their right to belong.

Perceptions about place can be highly subjective and frequently dependent upon memory, association, attitude or mood. The way we view and experience places can be very personal. What do we choose to notice? What are we being shown? Each individual brings their own story, and within a mixed family these stories and experiences can be more diverse. Members of any family unit are highly likely to experience places and events differently - consider the toddler, the teenage and the adult. Within a mixed cultural family differences in perception are more accentuated. The point where personal and cultural heritage meets the heritage of place (with all its breadth and depth of information) is where artists as facilitators can help to further personal understanding and expression.

The families experiences in the environment were made more memorable because they were shared with each other. Permission was given to bond with the physical landscape. In so far as all of us are people of place a mixed-heritage person is somebody who, literally or metaphorically, is someone of many places. In their memories and embodiment are traces of a multiplicity of landscapes. How do we negotiate this multiplicity of place to become present in the immediate environment? (Hurley, Gersie. 2014)[6]

The more I travel the more I love Britain, and it is because I love the place that I fight for my rights here.
Zephaniah. 2001[7]

Working Outside
...once children go outside and get stuck in, with little more than their imaginations, resourcefulness and a sense of fun they can have endless good times.
Schofield and Danks. 2011[8]

Most of the events were in beautiful countryside where people could freely play, relax, enjoy nature and socialize with each other. Intrinsic to the project were the positive benefits and known improvements to well-being that walking, playing and being outside bring.

Town and city were part of the trail and ideas for making a city walk are included. The workshops did not take place in outdoor centres and suitable locations had to be found for one-off workshops. We had to consider many aspects concerned with managing time, comfort, catering and family groups along with deciding what's possible creatively within the limitations.

How close were the sites to the river? were they safe and accessible for families? What was special about the landscape? Was it accessible by public transport? Was there a play and picnic area? What would the wet weather plan be? How far would we need to carry workshop materials and food? What are the catering arrangements going to be? It was a big ask for some families and a tall order for the artists and organisers.

Being in and connecting with the British countryside was a great leveller for a mixed cultural group. Everyone could enjoy connecting with the natural environment with many of the arts activities promoting a heightened awareness of the world around them. We spent time outside and we took time outside, the workshops were never rushed through.

The National Trust's 2012 'Natural Childhood Report' looked at children's connection to nature. The report asked whether people were disconnected from nature and they found a resounding YES for an answer. It identified some major barriers to children and families accessing the countryside as well as the importance to well-being and life learning of being outside in natural surroundings.

...ethnicity was also raised as a factor, with many telling us that minority ethnic groups felt increasingly isolated from nature and experienced this sense of isolation more than other groups.
National Trust 2012[9]

The report goes on to say that having a comparatively rural upbringing does not necessarily bring an automatic desire to spend time in nature.

Attitudes about the countryside vary considerably between cultures. Differences can include things like: living in the countryside as opposed to the city, attitudes towards camping, going for walks, entering woodland or approaching water and rivers.

Mixed families living in rural areas tend to be scattered and are therefore isolated geographically as well as socially and culturally. From the outside it is assumed that rural families access the countryside and green spaces, however this is often not the case. In this quiet corner of the country the needs of this generation of mixed children are easily overlooked.

Why Did We Do This?

Blazing Tales had worked with mixed-heritage families twice before with the Planet Rainbow Project. This project was a support service for mixed-heritage families, including those affected by trans-racial adoption, based in Exeter, Devon. The Planet Rainbow Project began in 2004 and after a struggle with funding it closed in 2010.

Blazing Tales first project was called 'Tail to Tale'. It was a series of workshops exploring stories from different cultures through song writing, visual-art and storytelling ending with the families performing their own story with full props, puppets and orchestra. 'Tail to Tale' was funded by the National Lottery and as it concluded The Planet Rainbow Project wanted to develop the partnership with Blazing Tales. Planet Rainbow workers had witnessed positive changes in people of all ages with increased confidence and self-esteem being a common outcome. The opportunity to build on our experiences provided opportunity to create appealing activities for the group.

Trust and relationships had been established and the company wanted to deepen their creative work and evaluate it more thoroughly. Blazing Tales felt it was important to reach for longer term collaborations, as well as for the artists to develop their combined arts working relationships, pushing against the one-off or short termism that can limit effectiveness for both artists and participants.

The Planet Rainbow Project wanted to work outside of the confines of an urban family centre and explore the hidden histories of the area whilst getting plenty of opportunity for outdoor play. Raising awareness and improving access for other mixed-heritage families who lived more rurally was also a key issue. The concept for the 'river exe-pedition' was Blazing Tales response.

As a lead-in to the longer project, and in preparation for taking the group on residential weekends, the Planet Rainbow Project and Blazing Tales led two long, autumn day, outdoor workshops finding the forgotten stories and lost songs based on the historical, global links of a significant local hill. These workshops proved successful in their own right and for the artists, participants and organisers alike paved the way for the river project

Mixed-Heritage Families

The project was aimed at people who share a dual, or multi-cultural experience within their families. A person is said to be of mixed-heritage if they have two, or more, different cultural heritages within them, commonly one black, Asian or white parent.

The Planet Rainbow Project described it like this:

Families with one 'black' or minority ethnic parent and one 'white' parent with mixed-heritage children. Families with a step parent who has a different ethnic background to the other parent/children. Families where both parents are either 'black' or minority ethnic or 'white', but have mixed-heritage backgrounds. Families that have adopted or fostered children from a different ethnic background, this is called trans-racial adoption.

Planet Rainbow 2007[10]

Naming

The debate around which terminology to use to describe 'mixed-ness' is a continuing and heated one. Different ways of describing 'mixed-ness' change alongside social and political changes and levels of acceptance. Most common self-referencing is mixed-race, mixed, dual-heritage, multi-heritage or the more American bi-racial. The fact is that there is no settled collective name. (Lincoln. 2011)[11]

Bradley Lincoln, from the organisation 'Mix-d' in Nottingham, says that the term 'mixed-heritage' is mostly used by academics and a study he ran with young people in Manchester found that they were most comfortable with being called 'mixed'. Language and naming is known to be driven forwards by young people before filtering into the mainstream.

Research by Dr Chamion Caballero has shown that most individuals and families prefer the more relaxed name 'mixed-race'. Finding words like heritage to be too removed or imposed upon them by politically correct professionals. (Caballero. 2010)[12]

At the start of this project the families already called themselves 'mixed-heritage' and were generally at ease doing so. Despite its verbal clumsiness this naming had become normalised. As the project had a leaning toward history the word 'heritage' had resonance. We interpreted heritage as being the cultural information informed by the experience of our upbringing combined with what we have inherited genetically. Within 'heritage' space is left to express individual cultural experiences and influences, accommodating complex cultural situations rather than just biological ethnicity. People's lives, families and circumstances are rarely straightforward and some people have complex cultural mixes within them. It is for these reasons that we have used the term mixed-heritage throughout this book.

Numbers

As Peter Aspinall points out, having the option to name yourself as mixed, and name your cultural heritage is a relatively recent option on the national census form.

For the first time in the 2000/01 national census round, census agencies in a number of Western countries offered options for people who, by virtue of their parentage or more distant ancestry, wished to declare a 'mixed' identity in questions on race and ethnic group... In 1991 the Great Britain Census had only provided free-text options for this population.
Aspinall. 2009[13]

Nationally, the mixed-heritage population went over one million people in the 2011 census for England and Wales. Showing a significant increase from 672,000 people who called themselves mixed in the 2001 census. From the 2011 statistics one third are mixed African-Caribbean and white followed by Asian and white. The Office for National Statistics[14] states that this is not a result of increasing birth rates but more that we are becoming less divided: the population is mixing up more.

One place with a high percentage of mixed families is the London borough of Haringey with a 4.4% mixed population. The whole of Devon averages as having a mixed population of 1.02%. This ranges from the lowest at 0.76% in West Devon to the highest in Exeter at 1.43% with most other districts around the 0.90% mark. It is clear to see from the whole national picture that there is a notable difference between the number of people who call themselves mixed who live in the major cities and those who live in the regions.

Mixed-Heritage Experience

Families come in all shapes, sizes and rainbow colours, with one or two parents, carers and one or several step parents. Any number of children are in their care, whether born to them, fostered or adopted. Family contact with extended family is equally varied. The majority of children and young people who attended were mixed and whose skin colour was a part of their story. It is important to state that for mixed-heritage families there is no single shared culture, faith, language, food, or experience.

The following text is from a 2007 paper 'Mixed families: assumptions and new approaches' written by Dr Chamion Caballero, a research fellow from The London South Bank University. It describes the breadth of experience within the 'mixed' population of Britain, based on research funded by The Joseph Rowntree Foundation.

The research emerging from the Joseph Rowntree Foundation project shows that there are certainly commonalities between the mixed families we spoke to.... For example, many of the families mentioned the importance of the area where they live on their experiences, the way they passed on their cultural heritages through food, as well as certain shared negative and positive reactions and assumptions of strangers - and sometimes family - to their mixedness. Yet, at the same time, our analysis is also starting to indicate that what may be helpful for developing a sense of belonging for children in one family's case - relationships with grandparents, geographical location, physical appearance, etc. - may be a hindrance for another family. For some, for example, relationships with grandparents are distant or problematic, but for others they provide a great source of support, not only practically but in helping children understand their cultural heritages. Similarly, those factors that may be helpful or a hindrance are not fixed, but may change over time. Moreover, the experiences of mixed families can be vastly different, not only between the type of mix, but within the mix itself. It is likely that parents with Jamaican and White British heritages may have a different approach or experience than a family with Chinese and White British heritages. Racism and prejudice take various forms, and these impact differently for different families.

Caballero 2007[15]

The above study was mostly of two parent families, whose experiences may no doubt be different to those of mixed lone parent families - indeed, it often appears to be mixed lone parent families that bear the brunt of … stereotypes and assumptions.

Prejudice and discrimination affect all members of minority groups and as Caballero also observes, …*persistent exposure to wrongful, ignorant or unkind behaviour damages one's sense of self-worth and inner dignity.* (in Schieffelin, Gersie & Nanson 2014)

Many manage the feelings this induces by adopting a single identity, like their 'mono-identified' peers, (Lincoln in Schieffelin, Gersie & Nanson 2014) or by shifting their allegiance across contexts. It is more balanced if mixed people can bring both sides of their cultural identity together and express an identity which is similar to but not specifically like either.

The Rural Mixed-Heritage Experience

The River Exe project brought these families together on the premise that living rurally is a hugely different experience from living in, and around, Britain's major cities. There is no intentional positive or negative bias to that statement, it's simply a fact. The 'Time for Action' report by Equality South West revealed that black, minority and ethnic (BME) individuals and households in rural areas feel isolated and without a voice. It also states that whilst urban racism and inter-communal tensions dominate public policy response, rural racism barely gets a look in.[16] The vast range of individuals that are known as BME includes mixed-heritage people. It's most common for mixed people to have one white parent which adds another layer of cultural complexity to the BME identification for them.

A high proportion of the participating families that brought themselves along to the events were white single mothers with mixed children, though not all and fathers from different ethnic backgrounds did participate. Whilst recognising the difficult reality of rural racism the project set out to provide a welcoming and creative meeting place where families could enjoy a shared experience. Individual stories of discrimination and stereotyping were able to be spoken about and ranged from the overt to the inadvertent.

Blazing Tales were interested to see what difference it made to families being with other families similar to their own, and how participating in creative activities affected them. Was it helpful for mixed children and families to relate to others like themselves? Being in a mixed-heritage family brings an extra dimension of negotiation to parenting and identity issues. It is evident that the majority of families share similar basic concerns.

In Devon's fields, lanes, market towns, sea-side and shores how connected do members of a mixed family feel to where they live? By looking beneath the superficial appearance of rural Britain a rich history of global connections, and constant change within its landscape, can be found; but they are often hidden away. The artists sought to develop this way of seeing beneath and beyond outward appearances. They sought feelings and connections to both 'here' and 'there' through acknowledgement of both.

It is easy to see the nature of a city or a country, just look and see the type of work that people are doing, look at the cars people drive, look at their houses, and look at the colour of their skins and how much money they spend. Get a guidebook or visit the tourist information office. It's so easy. But it's only part of the story. What really fascinates is what we can't see, what happens below the surface, who cleans up after us, and who dare not step up and be counted due to fear of either law makers or law breakers.

Zephaniah 2008[17]

As mixed families have no shared culture or in-built social reason to connect, opportunities for being together and sharing experiences are few and far between. In mostly rural regions they are scattered and socially isolated, mixed children and young people are frequently 'the only one', or in a tiny minority in the schools, villages and towns.

There is good reason to bring people in this circumstance together. Quite simply to be together in a place where they feel they don't have to explain themselves, for adults to talk and share experiences, for children to play together and see someone like them reflected back. Despite an apparent lack of commonality there appears to be an instant, mutual empathy between family members because a shared experience is recognised. One of the common factors is that the parents (present or not) generally speaking chose to mix with someone from another culture. On one hand (and probably at a personal level) - so what? It's no big deal. On the other hand inter-cultural marriage and love relationships have a relatively recent history of being illegal and socially frowned upon, even despised. It is an act that has seen family members disowned and these attitudes are still present in societies around the world. In 1964 inter-racial marriage was illegal in the United States and had a name that sounds like a disease - miscegenation.

Here was a group of people with a challenging collective history, who have had the courage to shift social boundaries and perceptions about mixed families. Mixed people do have a history and more work is currently needed to raise awareness about the history and ability to find out about it.

Meeting through arts activities proved an effective way to bring people together, being outside allowed all age groups dedicated time and space to build peer relationships, participate in creative self-expression and generally let off steam and play. Being with families in a similar situation, interacting and building friendships in a resonant place, connecting with it, discovering new information and contributing a new, creative response was intended to support a strengthening of mixed identity. The project sought to emphasise that all rivers lead around the world and remind participants that travel, trade and migration have been going on for hundreds and thousands of years.

The families journeyed through a changing landscape; near water that they lived by and water that had carried family members to and from distant shores, water that lay between met and unmet relatives, past, present and future water linking us all around the world. Moving down river encouraged a sense of moving forwards both externally and internally, all of which underpinned the creative arts workshops.

History

Devon's rich history reaches far and wide. By looking beneath the surface of local history it is possible to uncover stories about Devon's inter-cultural past and acknowledge the diversity of a region neighbouring the sea with a history of river trade. Acknowledging that people similar to themselves do have a history here, even if it is not well known. Knowing our story, where we are from, how we fit in and what our roots are can strengthen a sense of identity through our lives.

...migration is our nature...to be anti-migration is anti-nature...
Sissay 2013 [18]

Finding Hidden Histories

Local history is a piece of a giant jigsaw of a national story. That story, similarly, fits into a larger picture of world history.
Collicott. 1986[19]

In common with every place, Devon has historically sustained it's economy and population from it's available natural resources. Farming the land, fishing the sea, mining minerals and tending to animals - in Devon this was predominantly sheep. Dartmoor tin was traded with the Phoenicians in a large trading triangle from moor to sea and beyond from pre-Roman times. Wool had a place in human society since before recorded history. (Hoskins. 1954)[20] The whole region was a major world player in the wool and cloth industry from 12th Century through the Tudor period to 1700's, adapting to changing fashions and advances in weaving from rough kerseys to a finer cloth. Trade in and out of Exeter, Plymouth and Barnstaple reached around the world. Many world famous sea farers hailed from the area, Walter Raleigh, Humphrey Gilbert and Francis Drake to name a few. The south-west peninsula is well placed for global trade.

Devon has a history of farming fishermen and fishermen farmers, when work fell short in one they would take up the other. The path joining north Devon with south Devon was called The Mariner's Way, now similar to the Two Moors Way, was named for the sailors who travelled it in search of work. As today, sea faring is a multi-racial occupation and it's not only English sailors who would have trodden those paths. Women were also known to dress as men and work on board ship or in manual labour. An Exmouth woman, Anne Perriam, became nationally known as 'Warrior Woman' as she spent many years on board naval ships in the late 1700's working alongside her husband. (Gray. 2009)[21]

The history along the River Exe from Exford down to Exmouth is mostly one of moorland farming, sheep, wool and cloth production, with lowland husbandry, a provincial city with a mighty trading past, ending at the sea with an old port turned quiet seaside town. The river's history also features in the infamous fictional family of Lorna Doone (Blackmore. 1997)[22] on Exmoor and the powerful Courtenay family living at the estuary whose disputes over land and river access affected the building of the Exeter Canal.

Where can we find the hidden histories? How do we find the stories of the quiet people; the ones not valued or recorded? The stories of women, children, the poor or dispossessed, the immigrant or itinerant and the ordinary working person? The increasing desire to bring these stories into the main stream arose in the late 20th Century, rendering research into hidden histories a relatively new phenomena. Lucy MacKeith has explored the particularly difficult task of finding stories of 'black' people in her book Local Black History, A Beginning in Devon. (MacKeith 2003)[23]

Hidden history is a useful phrase because it shows that there is a story to be found. The reasons why it has been hidden are worth exploring, and can reflect past value systems and politics.

It is notable that the black and minority ethnic history of Britain goes largely unrecorded. This does not balance with what historians know about trade, travel and communication between nations over time. What has been recorded are things like imprisonment which tend to warp our knowledge and understanding of the past. Where there is no ready information does not mean that nothing happened there.
Gray 1999.[24]

To move towards a more accurate, inclusive view of history, we need to separate out the different elements which have been ignored previously. The evidence is available. The history waits to be written.
MacKeith. 2003

In 1999 Devon historian, Todd Gray instigated a black history project undertaken by 'The Friends of Devon Archives', because:

There was no principal collection of records and information was being gleaned from miscellaneous documents. It would take a single researcher years to find these sources.
Gray 1999.

Acknowledgement must be given to these researchers for making the information they have begun to uncover publicly available. For this project, local history with global links along the course of the River Exe was sought.

It is well known that the international wool trade played a hugely significant role in the story of the Exe, from the sheep farmers in the hills taking their wool into the city, then down for export at the major ports of Exeter and Topsham. Exeter and Topsham (a small town on the estuary) have both enjoyed international recognition as powerful centres of commerce that belie their size and rural charm. Topsham was famed around the world for it's ship building until the early 1800's.

These ports were part of the Atlantic highway for trade of which cod was a main commodity in the 17th and 18th century; Newfoundland cod was exchanged for Spanish and Portuguese wine; from the late 1600's sugar was imported and refined here; up until the 1900's even guano (bird droppings) was imported from South America for use as a miracle fertiliser. Wool, cotton, fish, spices, metals and much more, were bought, sold and exchanged around the world during these centuries. British products of coal, slate, lime, chalk and tin, for example, were exported from Topsham down the Exe estuary and out into the Channel. (Topsham Museum and St Nicholas Priory, Exeter.)[25]

In an age long before the Elizabethan discovery of new worlds, Exeter had been the administrative centre for the Romans, and tin was traded with the Greeks around the 4th century. In 2001, the discovery on Dartmoor of the Whitehorse Hill Burial showed a pre-historic cremation, over 4,000 years old, where astonishingly preserved grave goods included beads from other countries.

...the number and variety of beads is astonishing with the amber having most probably originated form the Baltic area. When all of the beads were strung, they must have formed a magnificent necklace.
Marchand, 2013/14 [26]

People have always traded and inter-mingled, for better or worse, and it is not possible to talk about international trade links during the 17th and 18th centuries without mention of the Atlantic slave trade.

The slave trade and slavery are not the only parts of Devon's history where we can find black people. But the contribution from black people in slavery, especially to the wealth of some people in Devon, is significant. (MacKeith. 2003)

Devon did not have the history of slavery that places like, Bristol had, though wealthy families were heavily involved with the sugar trade in the West Indies and America, for example. One of the most well-known slaves, and later abolitionist, was Olaudah Equiano who writes about spending time with his friends in both Exeter and Plymouth in his autobiography which was first published in 1789 by Olaudah Equiano or Gustavus Vassa, The African[27]. There is a famous portrait in the Royal Albert Memorial Museum, Exeter, of 'An Unknown African' that was thought to have been Equiano. The portrait is used on the cover of the 2003 Penguin Classics edition however nobody seems to know and the mystery remains unsolved.

Later in his life Equiano married an English woman, Susanna Cullen, and they had two daughters. This happened in Cambridgeshire, but is worth mentioning because it is a significant part of mixed history. His first daughter, died at the age of 4 years old. It appears that the family were respected in Chesterton, and this inscription can still be read in St. Andrew's Church. This is part of it,

...Know that there lies beside this humble stone
A child of colour, haply not thine own.
Her father born of Afric's sun-burnt race,
Torn from his native field, ah foul disgrace:
Through various toils, at length to Britain came
Espoused, so Heaven ordain'd, an English Dame...
Osborne. 2007[28]

Equiano's second daughter married a reverend who was living in Appledore, in North Devon, at the time. After the marriage, she joined him and they lived there for four or five years. There are no known accounts of what life was like for her as a woman of African and English heritage in early 19th century Britain, or how they were treated as a couple. (Torrington. 2007)[29]

Another early account of a mixed marriage in Devon took place in Moretonhampstead in 1808 when a black servant of a French officer married a local girl, Susanna Parker.

The bells rang merrily all day. From the novelty of this wedding being the first negro ever married in Moreton, a great number assembled in the churchyard, and paraded down the street with them.
That year there was also a terrible fire in Moretonhampstead.
It was pleasing to see about 1,500 people of different languages and colours uniting with great cheerfulness in making breaches to stop the progress of the flames.
MacKeith 2003

The historical information we were looking for focused on the area around the River Exe, which excluded some richer seams of information. Here, I cite a few, short fragments of stories from along the river which point towards the various dynamics of inter-cultural histories. These stories are of their time and can appear culturally patronising, any record of slavery is certainly painful to remember.

There is one notable story of trans racial adoption from the late 1800's in the Exe estuary town of Topsham. The Scottish United Presbyterian missionary, Mary Slessor dedicated her life to working in the Calabar region of West Africa (today's Nigeria) where she took in and provided homes for twins that had been abandoned in the forest.

In Calabar at the time, the birth of twins was treated with suspicion: the Efik people feared twins and such babies were usually killed or cast aside to die.
Ayres 2013[30]

In 1882 Mary Slessor rescued an infant girl called Atim Eso whom she later adopted and gave the name Janie. Janie stayed with Mary for the rest of her life, travelling with her between Calabar and the U.K. In 1885 and 1891 Mary Slessor rented properties in Topsham. Mary quickly became involved with village and church life and Janie was known to accompany her. Hand written correspondence in Topsham Museum shows that Janie was remembered as a little child visiting the women of the town. Janie was said to have spoken with a Dundee accent having spent much of her life in Scotland. (Ayres 2013)

Mary and Janie also spent long periods in Africa. Mary lived with the Okoyong people for fifteen years and eventually became known as the 'White Queen of Okoyong'. She died in a remote part of Nigeria in 1915 at the age of 66. To mark her death flags were flown at half-mast in Lagos where she received the colonial equivalent of a state funeral. (Ayres 2013)

In Todd Gray's, 'The Victorian Under Class of Exeter' he brings to attention a collection of reports written by a journalist who visited the Exeter work house in 1854. In them he describes meeting Dahlia Graham in the aged-women's-ward.

We approached and observed one old lady seated in a cane-wrought chair with considerable ease and dignity......Around her head was bound a many coloured kerchief, in that fantastic style that obtains in tropical climates.
Gray 2001[31]

Dahlia had been kidnapped in Senegal at an early age and later sold by a West-Indian slave-dealer to an Exeter family who owned plantations in the West Indies. She served the family for twenty years and was rewarded for her service by being sent to the workhouse where the reporter says she 'rejoiced' in the standard of her living conditions. Having survived kidnap and the middle passage Dahlia ended her days in Exeter, she was 93 at the time of this meeting.

The image below from 1871 shows the daughter of an English merchant in West Africa on a visit to Exeter. Judging by her clothes and the fact she was accompanying her father on a trip, I assume that this girl was treated with more regard than many children like her at the time. Part of the mixed-heritage story from this era is of white slave owners raping and impregnating the black female slaves in their possession. This was followed by varied attitudes from the fathers towards their children, with no acknowledgment being most the common.

(Grey. 2003)[32]

Moving continents and switching focus to India leads to mentioning the early days of the East India Company and the Devon, Palk family.

Robert Palk was born in 1717 to a modest farming family living near south Dartmoor. He went on to be a wealthy and prominent figure handling the affairs of the East India Company. His enormous wealth and status were gained as part of the 'Drain of Wealth' that saw India impoverished. Robert Palk's family carried serge from the cloth mills near his home over the Haldon Hills to Exeter to trade. Palk later bought Haldon House, a stately home, and in 1788 he commissioned the building of the Haldon Belvedere. This is an ornate triangular tower built on the prominent Haldon Hills that overlook Exeter and can be seen for many miles around. (Fraser. 2008)[33]

Intrepid researchers have begun to make inroads into the story of black people in Devon, and there is undoubtedly more to uncover. Within the constraints of my research I have found less history about Indian people or those from other countries and continents. The families involved in the river exe-pedition were hoping that we would find some early stories about mixed relationships or families along our route. Before the arrival of 'war babies' in World War Two no stories seem to have come to light. The stories are there, they are waiting to be found.

The geographical position of our area in relation to the rest of the world has everything to do with its stories. With sea to the north and south and the river we were following running practically through its middle this place has many stories to tell with global connections. Its southern coast leads naturally out into the Atlantic Ocean, and as a once larger than life colonial empire and birth place of Tudor explorers this small island was all too well known around the world.

The coast of Devon and Cornwall was equally inviting to arriving raiders and attackers as it was to the departing Britains. The year 1625 saw large numbers of ships destroyed and West Country people captured as slaves by the Islamic corsairs of Barbary. In that year the mayor of Plymouth reported 1,000 skiffs lost and a similar number taken into slavery. (Milton. 2004)[34] The coming decades saw repeated attacks on Devon and Cornwall with many men, women and children being taken into slavery in Morocco.

With Devon's history of sea-faring, fisherman and sailors were constantly at risk of kidnap by pirates for many centuries. Some communities were said to keep ransom funds and this kind of financial safe-guard is pivotal to the Dartmoor folk-tale of 'Benji's Ghost'.

The folk tale is set inland on the northern edge of Dartmoor in a town not far from the Mariner's Way. The people were farmers but when times were hard they would go to the sea in search of work. The Benji in the story was Benjamin Gayer, Mayor of Okehampton and he was in charge of the town's ransom fund. The community contributed what money they could to a fund that could be used to pay off the pirates should their men ever be captured at sea. Benjamin Gayer decided to invest the ransom cound he guarded and he lost all the money. Times did become hard in town and the farmers walked the Mariner's Way. Shortly after they put to sea they were kidnapped by pirates. The Okehampton families who were left behind went to the mayor to ask to use the fund to bring back their loved ones only to find it spent, the town had lost its men. The wives, children, parents and grandparents of the kidnapped men vented their grief and rage on Benji who collapsed and died. After his death his ghost could find no rest, he tormented the townsfolk with terrible wailing. To this day he is said to still haunt nearby Cranmere Pool, where he is condemned to forever empty its waters with a sieve.

The Moor and the sea, those great twin spirits of Devon, abound with ghostly tales of days of gone by.
Day Sharman. 1952 [35]

Storytelling

The ground holds the memory of all that has happened to it. The landscape is rich in story. The lives of our ancestors and our remote ancestors have contributed to the shape and form of the land we know today...

Lupton. 2007 [36]

This project sought stories that were rooted in the place as well as bringing stories to influence its evolution. As with the richness of its history the area is teeming with folk tales, myths, legends and tales of memorable characters. Exe specific stories were looked for and stories from around the world that touched upon themes for the group. However, unlike the Exe's sister: The River Dart, and Exmoor's cousin: Dartmoor whose stories and histories are prolific, the Exe stories did not reveal themselves so easily.

A string of fascinating outsiders came to light: Exmoor highwayman Tom Faggus, his dwelling was never known and he shod his horses shoes on backwards so it looked like he was coming when he was going and going when he was coming; of Princess Carabou; a village girl who successfully presented herself as an exotic princess for many years; of Bampfylde Moore Carew born the son of a vicar and who died The King of the Gypsies. These fascinating people were born near the river, lived close to it all their lives and some were buried beside it. Despite being born and bred Devon people they moved between worlds and never fully part of mainstream Devon customs and society.

It undoubtedly matters to awaken historical imagination and knowledge. It is, however, wrong to assume that the main connection between storytelling, stories and place concerns site-specific storytelling....where people receive storied information linked with that site. Throughout the world storytellers use place in stories and tell stories about places for many more reasons than providing information or creating happier citizens. Moreover they do so to listeners who rarely compose an homogenous group. In Britain particularly, storytelling audiences are often heterogeneous with regard to individual age, ethnic background, class, level of education and story preference. The rich diversity also affects the listener's experience and expectations as well as the teller's practise with regard to storytelling, stories and place.

Gersie. 2010 [37]

Story was a part of the multi-layering of this project and a cumulative experience for the participants. A part of their own making-sense from the locations visited, creative activities chosen and relationships developed. Everyone came from a different place or perspective especially bearing in mind the range of ages. Everyone had their own perceptions of the story of their journey.

And we, the people, treading the skin of the world beneath the vast dome of its sky, we are its dreams.

Lupton, 2007

Blazing Tales' Approach to Mixed-Heritage

The participants are families with no shared culture and a wide age difference all of whom have 'a subtle lived experience'. (Lincoln. 2011) They are being led by three white British artists, one of whom has mixed children, aiming to democratically engage the youngest to the oldest. They are in not-for-purpose, once visited, outside locations near water in possession of a crazy idea!

Families came for a good day out somewhere new, for their children to play together and to do some interesting creative things in the environment. The rest was osmosis, in the background, gathering momentum with the strength of the river, flowing towards making sense and storing memories.

As with many applied arts projects there is an issue to be explored, to become more understood and here it is about being in a mixed family, or being a mixed child or young person living in a rural region. By the nature of the whole situation it was not appropriate to constantly headline the issue. There was a balance to be struck between parents with a strong desire to talk about it and those who were vaguely interested. Between letting young children simply be themselves, in supporting young people to develop a positive attitude to their identity and supporting those who didn't – currently - want to think about being mixed heritage. It required considerable decision making and flexibility to try and meet differing needs. The artists leading a self-referring group were respectful of individual's stories and cannot ask about, or interfere with, private lives. They were mindful of learning where and how future work with the families, or just the children and young people could best be taken forward.

The artists initiated combined activities to stimulate and provoke creative responses. They were managing the subtle balance between encouraging what is in you to come out with providing new information and ideas. Meeting people on their own terms whilst showing them a door they could go through if they wanted to. Stories, individuality and culture emerge through the invitation of creativity and the opportunities for self-expression were made all the more vital by being time, place and group specific. The arts activities provided the framework for the outside events, around which people shared personal stories and younger children played and connected in a way that did not prick their consciousness or make them feel 'other'. (Hurley in Schieffelin, Gersie & Nanson 2014) Relaxing into a feeling of 'us' was a kind of cultural validation. On the evaluation form we asked the adults questions about the heritages in the family, but for the younger children we chose not to ask specific questions about being mixed.

A family support worker was present at each event. Parminder Southcott, who was experienced in mixed-heritage family work and is mixed-heritage herself, was the ideal person to help bridge the relationship between the artists and families. Part of her role was to actively encourage and develop formal and informal conversations about mixed-ness, without initiating any, to chair talking times when they happened and offer support and guidance to family members if and when it was needed.

Each workshop referenced British and another culture. The company was not inspired by the idea of holding different cultural days or only doing traditional, cultural crafts. The cultural conundrum of mixed-ness is not necessarily met by that approach, especially for younger participants who might want a more contemporary approach reflecting their current, mixed experiences.

Part Two
The Workshops

Like a River

Like a river I meet different people

Like a sea I go to different places

Like the water-cycle we sometimes have to start all over again

Like a tributary we see each other in all sorts of places

Like a stream we have to say our goodbyes

Olivia M. Aged 10. written in Exford.

(With kind permission of the author.)

Exford

'Songs and Spring'

Inside the Metaphor

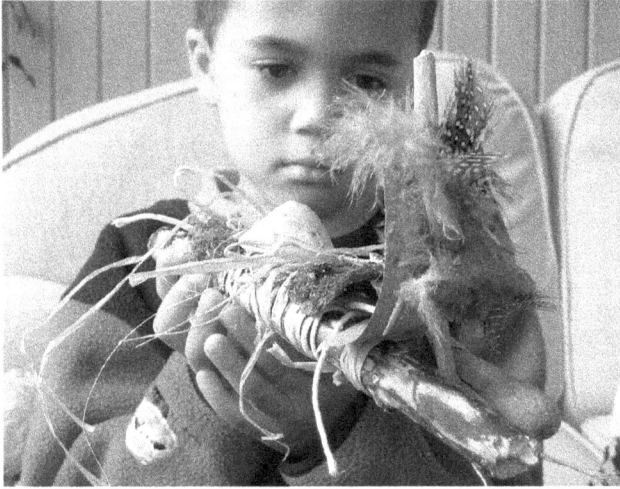

The whole weekend had a real community feeling with everyone working together and producing art in various forms. I valued meeting people in similar circumstances who my child and I could feel totally natural with.

Snowdrops carpeted the ground and Exmoor was covered in brittle, brown bracken and bare trees. We had hired Exford Youth Hostel for the weekend, 14 families came to stay and met the young River Exe flowing at the bottom of the garden.

This residential weekend was held together through song. Song making started on the first night where lyrics evolved as people contributed stories of their journey to Exford. The following morning a second song, 'The Beginning' was initiated. This atmospheric piece was about the start of things and Hugh writes about this in his chapter. Writing, developing and playing the songs punctuated the whole weekend between other activities.

In the morning we made boats from natural sources and beach driftwood we had brought with us. Poetry inspired by the place and the metaphor of the river was written. In the afternoon we took a long walk along the

River Barle, to Tarr Steps and beyond. At night in the pitch, moor black we led a night walk. Before bed there was a participatory story and singing session that the younger children hugely enjoyed.

To close the weekend the boats were set sail, poems shared and songs sung including a new, goodbye song called 'Words on a Boat'. The group spent a while on the river bank, children paddling in wellies as their boats began the long journey down river. Would we see them again further downstream or washed up on the shore at Exmouth?

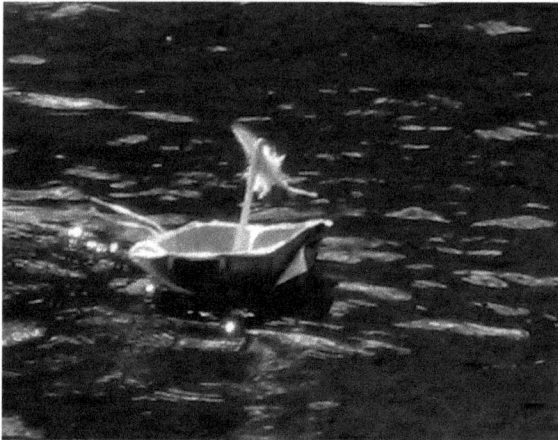

High Exe Valley

'Indigo and Buddleia'

Having time and space

This weekend and other times like this are invaluable for me as the white parent of a mixed heritage child for support and interaction and relaxation and for my daughter to be in an open and accepting environment.

This workshop was a summer residential camping weekend on a farm-come-nature reserve with no livestock situated in the Exe Valley. The river was a short walk away coursing through a wood sided valley where the scenery is stunning and the wildlife vibrant. The farm has spacious camping terraces, central fire pit, a large tent for inside gatherings with a wood burner, an open sided, canvas roofed area, an outdoor kitchen, compost toilets and basic, but innovative, washing arrangements.

Main meeting terrace

Some local history

The farm is situated east of Tiverton, a town known as a centre for wool and cloth for centuries. The town's wealth comes from this trade, and beneficiaries have historically donated buildings to the town from wealth gained in this way: from Peter Blundell and John Greenaway in medieval times through to the arrival of John Heathcoat in 1861. Heathcoat set up mills in Tiverton that mirrored the Nottingham area townscapes where he had grown up. Heathcoat Factory lace has adorned the wedding dresses of queens, and the factory is still a main employer today.

Enjoying the woods

The Exe has been a significant contributor to the success of the wool and cloth industry and Tiverton's town crest represents this history clearly. The river and wool sack are central to the crest, both vital factors to the growth of the market town and the sustenance of its people. It was introduced by King Edward III (1327-77) and was stuffed with English wool as a reminder of England's traditional source of wealth, the wool trade, as a sign of prosperity.

Tiverton Town Crest

The Global Connection

The cloth industry exported and imported its goods and throughout history trade peaked and troughed with various countries and continents. Nearer to home there were links with France and the Netherlands with trade also reaching as far as China, Africa, India and the Middle East.

Our intention was to 'tip a wink' at the history of the place and look at its reliance on water from the river. Whilst discovering what the group brought to the place and made happen there, our thread in a continuing story of new experiences.

Blazing Tales creative response to this location.

How the place affected our creative decisions?

We decided to lead a textiles based activity using different methods of dyeing. Cara had specialised in the art of dyeing and her interpretation for this project was to use dyes and patterning techniques from Britain and around the world.

On the first evening the families went off in groups around the site to collect dye plants, with instructions about which plants gave what colour and what not to eat. That evening the plants were brewed up and the prepared wool and cloth were put on to brew. The following day a vat of green indigo dye was introduced and other dyeing methods experimented with. Indigo is a dye of great cultural importance in the Middle East, China, Japan and Africa: a huge mass of the earth's surface.

Some people turned their fabric into bags, made buttons and experimented with colour, sewing and different materials. Hugh and Sara took their cue from the visual art stimulus and developed spin off activities to mix with these ideas.

Visual Arts workshop aims:

1.   To identify and pick plants from the site and prepare them for dyeing on wool.

2.   To learn how to dye and pattern cloth using Indigo.

3.   To introduce the Japanese patterning technique, Shibori, amongst other techniques, including batik and tie dye.

4.   To make bags and wall hangings, also making buttons from wood.

Indigo dyeing

Brewing Dragon Soup

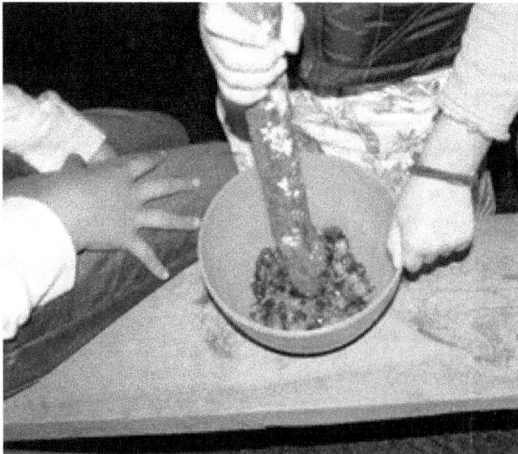
Making pink

Old buddleia for yellow

Indigo dyed fabric

Using a tjanting to draw in wax

A song was composed by the group around the evening fire as the dye pot brewed:

O we're making Dragon Soup, in a great big group
Underneath the stars, the Dragon Soup is ours!!

Collecting the plants on the first evening worked well on a number of levels. It was a welcoming, fun opportunity for people to get to know the site and each other, either re-connecting or meeting for the first time. The group were interested in finding out about the plants, their dye colours and plant identification, so the activity was also a nature quiz. The children enjoyed preparing the plants, mixing and mashing, they were given clear supervision about poisonous plants, such as Yew.

Like sorcerers we made different pots of brew, put them on the fire and shared supper. After a fire-side supper we sang to the dye pots, laughed, sang songs and told stories into the night.

There was huge excitement the following morning when we first saw the result of the Dragon Soup; the marvellous gold that was produced from the old buddleia flower heads. We all knew that singing under the stars around the fire had helped!

Music workshop aims:

Hugh is not generally one for singing existing songs, but he'd learnt 'Mood Indigo' by Duke Ellington especially for the project which he then taught to the group. The instruments he'd brought were hand chimes and small percussion. His accompanying instruments were accordion and guitar.

Hugh writes new songs and this is how he did it on this occasion. The artists help each other out with their lead activities and once the indigo dyeing was well underway Hugh invited people to join him gathering lyrics. They were asked to go around the group asking individuals to give a line for the song. All were engrossed in a visual art activity which has its own calm intensity. The resulting song became a fascinating, personalised glimpse into the arts process.

Staggering the flow of activities supported the different age groups and gave space for differing amounts of sewing and dyeing depending on skills and interest. The music picked up from the art while the art followed on from the stories. When the art making was finished, or if people needed a break, they could drop in on music making, or go off to rest or play. A core group of music makers was established who experimented with sounds and began composing. They continued throughout the weekend with others dropping in and out.

Hand chimes are very inclusive in music making. Rather like bell ringing one person has one note to play which contributes to the whole sound. Three year olds stood next to adults, each knew their position and time to ring and both sounded equal to the ear.

The music provided an orchestral score for the weekend. As white cloths were dipped in the indigo vat we sang Ella Fitzgerald's lyric's to 'Mood Indigo'. The new song 'Come Dye With Me', held in it the quality of the experience becoming a shared and much loved anthem by the end. It wholly belonged to the group, being a song about their collective experience which was composed by the group for the group.

Hugh wrote one to one songs with some children during quiet times, each song giving a snapshot of what they were talking or thinking about at the time. Later the whole group learnt these songs and sang them.

Storytelling workshop aims:

With night falling, stars coming out and dye pots brewing over a glowing fire the families settled in for their first night's camp and the singing and stories began. The traditional story which linked the arts activities for the weekend was called How Indigo came to Devon. It had been told to Sara by Clive Fairweather who first knew the story as How Indigo came to Ireland.

On the first telling of the weekend the two main characters, a farmer and a sea captain, were both from Devon and the action was set in a pub in Tiverton. However, inspired by the events of the weekend the background of the characters and their settings evolved whilst the bones and content of the story remained as originally passed on.

The indigo dyeing happened the day after the storytelling. It provoked childhood memories for one of our fathers. As he sewed, designing his pattern, he recalled visiting his grandparents indigo business in Iran and spoke about what he had seen and experienced there. His grandparents were the last in a long heritage of indigo dyers who had their own secret dye recipes and specialist designs.

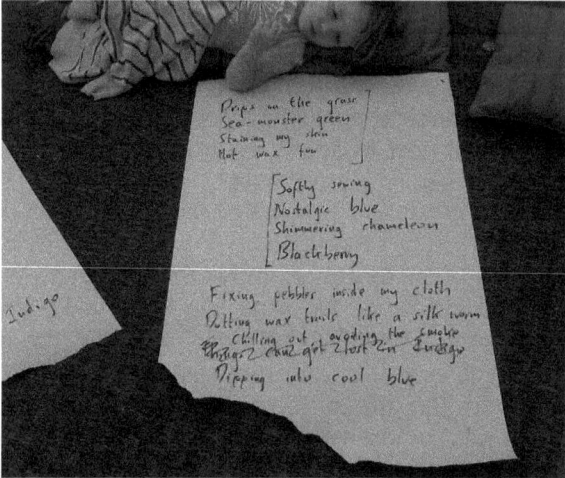

Indigo song lyrics

The story changed to show how a Tiverton farmer and an Iranian sea captain struck a bargain which led to indigo becoming available to the weavers and dyers of Devon, and came to be set in a pub on Exmouth dock. Imaginative around the edges, it provided an insight into global trade links. As the indigo is introduced here, the Iranian sea-captain takes wool, serge and tin to trade down the Atlantic coast on his way to Morocco and beyond.

One afternoon we held a story making walk. After some improvisation and word games the group learnt more about the history of the area. Sara aimed to make this into a vibrant, relevant story rather than giving a local history talk. From her research she had devised four 'Story Starters'. These nuggets of historical truth act as springboards into a narrative which could become a short poem, a long story, a song or an image. The group were introduced to the Story Starters before they set off on an exploratory walk toward the river.

They decided, in pairs, small groups or solo, which story they'd like to find out more about before leaving. Everyone had notebooks and pencils, sticky strips and collecting bags. They were asked to find clues and ideas in the landscape that would inform their story. The aim was to explore and to find information or ideas which would help to develop the stories rather than fixing meaning or consequences at this stage.

People enjoyed the workshop and the story making walk, some went on to develop their findings into stories and songs.

Notes from Sara's journal: *I hope this gives something of Devon's history, that is made real by having the opportunity to imagine it as happening in the landscape – in these places – and that the scenarios are easy for young people, and adults, to identify with and begin ideas.*

Time and space

The activities flowed on one from the other, relationships entered new phases over three days, becoming more relaxed and familiar as group dynamics and routines settled in. Being outside in a wonderful natural environment started to take effect, it was a welcome holiday. A large part of the success of the weekend was due to there being enough time and space to explore ideas, relationships between people and with the landscape.

Participants were not rushed through activities and the facilitators had time to attend to the natural flow of the group. There was space to do as much or as little as felt comfortable, with opportunity to go off and play either with, or away from family members which suited all age groups and needs.

Story synopsis

How Indigo came to Devon.

A farmer and a sea-captain meet in a pub and get talking about whether a person gets on best in life if they follow their instincts and do what they were born to do, or if it's best for them to train and learn new skills. An argument ensues and a bet is placed. The sea-captain bets a shipment of indigo and the farmer bets his cattle.

The cards are called for and the game begins. During the card game the sea-captain pulls out a cat from his bag and sits it on the table. He orders the cat to sit up and places a candle between the cat's paws. As the short-legged table rocks from side to side the cat sways but the candle remains alight and not one drop of wax is dropped. The captain has taught the cat to hold the candle so they can play cards on their long nights at sea. In this way the sea-captain has proved that to get on best in life new skills must be learnt.

The farmer is dejected, he returns home to tell his wife. He is scared as to how she will react but she is compassionate and has an idea. The next day they both prepare the cattle for the journey to meet the sea-captain. The farmer and sea-captain meet again and the sea-captain strokes his cat and feels pleased with himself for winning the farmer's cattle.

The farmer walks up to the sea-captain, puts his hand in his pocket and draws out a mouse which he sets down on the ground. Inevitably, the cat gives chase and the farmer has the last word in showing that you have to follow your instincts and do what you were born to do. In this way the farmer wins the shipment of indigo and introduces it to the weavers and dyers of Devon.

Preparing dye

Cara Roxanne's Tale
Visual arts

My role, as artist, was to add a visual response to the places we visited along the river. Investigating the history, stories and landscape of the area enabled me to develop ideas for a variety of artistic stimuli to help guide the participants on their journey visually.

During my early twenties I spent a few years studying plant dyes, a vast and fascinating subject. This project seemed an ideal opportunity to re-visit this ancient craft and explore colour. Investigating local plant dyes provided an opportunity to learn about the plants found in Britain and specifically along the River Exe. As we were connecting with the river I particularly wanted to find a pigment that would represent the focus of water. Indigo seemed perfect as it is a major cold water dye. Dip dyeing with local plant dyes and imported indigo from the southern hemisphere was a combination steeped in association: an intrinsic link to Exeter's vast wool and cloth industry which linked Devon to the world through trade.

It is hard to sum up the significance of indigo. It has been the most important dye in the world, its history and legacy is vast and it's colour far reaching. From the dye used on ceremonial clothes throughout Africa, to the initial dye source for the world's most famous jeans distributor Levi's. Jenny Balfour-Paul's book Indigo (2011)[1] is a valuable resource into the influence of indigo on the world.

My approach as a visual arts facilitator

Process

The process of dyeing reflected my approach to facilitating a group creatively. Although I have practical knowledge of process, my role was to guide rather than teach, enabling others to explore, play and ultimately express themselves freely. A perfect product outcome was not the aim. Instead I was supporting a collective leap into the unknown, focusing on the journey we made together, or alone.

For the first part of the process participants ventured into the surrounding landscape to identify and collect plants that could be used for dyeing. The gathering of the plant dyestuffs provided a focus for the group forays.

Each of them explored the landscape differently: some climbed trees; others enjoyed a leisurely stroll or shared memories of childhood while some recounted knowledge of medicinal uses of particular plants. Each individual experience was different but participants and facilitators alike began to deepen their relationship with the landscape and each other.

Some people returned with lots of materials, others with a few. Their contribution to the dye process was ultimately not as important as their experiences outdoors. Providing a theme and loose structure to their time outside encouraged each person to find their own relationship with the environment.

This method of working was echoed when participants were sewing and applying batik processes to their cloth. I laid out various materials and tools, guiding participants in possible ways of using them, encouraging everyone to play and try out new techniques without being fixed to a specific template. Each person followed their own interests within the theme and was able to chat comfortably about discoveries and processes whilst working.

Space

Whether working inside or outside it is always constructive to create a place for a group to connect to the theme of a workshop and each other, through key visual stimuli and equipment. Preparation is vital, as is the recognition that it takes time and effort to carefully create a space for others to work in. For example changing the layout and design in a classroom can help a class re-imagine the space. Or when investigating a particular subject using props, tools and pictures that can be seen, touched, and even used will help motivate and engage participants; hopefully inspiring a wealth of invention and imagination.

Chance and coincidence

When leaping creatively into the unknown, the unexpected elements of chance or coincidence can occur. During the weekend we dyed cloth, one member of our group brought this clearly to life. His grandparents in Iran were the last of a lineage whose profession was built on indigo. The family had had their own secret indigo dye recipe which had been used to dye tiles. It was a surprise for both him and us that he had arrived at an arts workshop to find he was exploring a medium so fundamental to part of his own heritage.

A true moment of the unexpected is when 'something goes wrong', no matter how small the mistake or problem is. Some of the best pieces of art, music or even scientific discoveries have been made when the maker has done something accidentally. This unexpected error or 'happy accident' then leads in an entirely new direction, opening doors to further exploration and expression. Sometimes sad happenings can turn out positively, for example: when Matisse could no longer paint, because of ill health he began instead cutting paper and working with blocks of colour. In the process he created some of his most prominent work and his famous picture book 'Jazz'. (Matisse. 1998)[2]

Dyeing is a beautiful, fascinating artform which in skilled hands can produce almost perfect designs. Rather than focus on creating perfect designs the workshop provided an opportunity to mirror the beauty of the natural world in all its variations. Dyeing cloth, along with many creative processes, challenges people's desire to control situations. It is rather like planning to have a particular kind of child and then discovering the baby, once born, is different and absolutely their own self! It's impossible to tell how each piece of cloth will react to the plant's dye. The time of year, amount of sun on the plant, hardness of the water and many other factors contribute to the individual differences that can occur each time a cloth is dyed. These beautiful 'imperfections' are a glorious contrast to the stark world of factory-made perfection. Plant dyes give a sense of the place and story of origin behind their colour. They are a colourful, wonderful expression of humans and plants working together.

Environmental art

For artists working outdoors there can be a seemingly endless amount of materials to use and play with. The ideas of artists such as Richard Long and Andy Goldsworthy have become dominant in many types of outdoor response. Finding innovative ways to utilize natural materials to create new art forms is an exciting challenge. There can be a transient beauty to working with many natural materials, as such creations may not survive for long in their location. Whilst echoing the changing landscape, by working with natural materials we are trying to create something of beauty which does not disturb the land we are drawing from and returns something to it.

Production.

The fantastic process of artists working together creates products which resonate as well as combining different artistic media. For example, participants didn't just leave the residential weekend with a handmade indigo-and-plant-dyed bag, the bag was filled with memories: of walks, conversations, giggles and frustrations, of songs sung and crafts learnt, a bag which has sewn into its seams memories of a friend they met during the weekend, a bag which holds both history and myths of indigo's arrival to Devon and a bag which has in its fabric the mysterious conception of colour.

Cara

A musician, a storyteller and a visual artist.

It was a great opportunity to work alongside other artists. Working together as a team we deepened our creative relationship, exploring ways to seek a communal vision instead of an individual focus. Working closely together meant that we could never entirely plan our work beforehand as so much was open to how members of the group reacted to the activities, weather conditions, chance and how our activities and ideas supported one another in actuality. For example, whilst plant dyes were dipped in a vat of inky green indigo, alchemical songs were crafted and sung with Hugh. Sara told stories while people sewed and worked on their creations, again adding layers of texture and meaning to their work.

By working as a team we let go of any individual person's vision and the creative focus was supported by each member of the group. Together everyone involved discovered a natural way of working and playing together, effortlessly sharing and flowing through art forms.

The River Bank Day
'Swallows and Crocodiles'
Choosing and using a location.

Location

This was the first full day workshop which ran from 11.00am – 6.00pm. This location was very difficult to find and location is all important when leading outside workshops because it affects the whole experience. From personal comfort, safety and considerations of accessibility through to being able to engage with the place, play and be creative. The location also had to be private enough and not disturb other people, animals or risk trespass.

Many maps were checked and dead end walks done before we located a stretch of river that could be walked along and parked nearby which was suitable for families of mixed age and ability to spend a relaxing day out. In the end it offered local families an opportunity to explore somewhere most had never been, yet was very close to where they lived and easily accessible by public transport.

From the village we walked down the path to a series of well-worn earth paths that lead along the river's edge. It's a pastoral scene of flat, grazing fields on a flood plain. A meandering river with pied flycatcher (look like a swallow but smaller) filled banks and hedgerows with a church spire beyond. The main line train runs parallel to the river. The whole area has public access, is signposted and is a popular spot for walking dogs, picnicking or swimming.

Some history

The local history of this location seemed to be similar to that up stream of farming, wool and cloth. No significant local personalities, myths or legends were discovered during our research in preparation for the day.

Global connection.

Therefore, the focus for the workshop was on bringing ourselves and our stories to the river and creating a little piece of history there. This was done through provocations into personal stories during the workshop and by responding to a Pacific story about a crocodile and a golden cloth which linked with the river and connected to the previous workshop themes about cloth.

By bringing this story to the river bank we were playing with the idea of overlaying an experience on a place. Looking at what happens to perception and memory when the location is enlivened through storytelling and arts activities. The broad aim underpinning the day was to explore what other influences we bring to a place and how our stories contribute to, enhance and amplify it's story.

Blazing Tales creative response to this location.

How the place affected our creative decisions.

It is vital to make a pre-visit as a team to prepare for the smooth and safe running of a workshop. A thorough health and safety check is mandatory and it's important to be aware of the kind of things to look out for when preparing to work outside. Anticipating a long list of what might go wrong in a location is often the best way to do this. It is invaluable for an artist to see where they are being asked to work as this allows for alternative strategies to have been anticipated; which is essential when best made plans have been laid to rest. However site visits are also stimulating, productive and inspiring and this visit sparked ideas and plans about the details of the day.

The artists visited the surrounding area in the company of the idea and a story. The geography, facility and materials at the site supported, and heavily influenced, the planning for the day. The shape of the workshop formed as the natural resources available to us and the best place to set up camp became clear. Sara told the story, Hugh thought of an Indonesian song he knew and decided to bring his gong collection, Cara saw that something could be made from the natural objects found in the place. We decided to include the idea of 'special things' to our workshop planning as a way of encouraging personal storytelling within a framework.

Since visiting Exford and coming across a Penny Tree we had wanted to begin one further downstream. A Penny Tree is a fallen dead tree that people hammer pennies into whilst making wishes to fairy folk who will hopefully grant them. A good tree was present here.

At each location something unexpected arose that needed responsible handling by the leaders and participants. On this occasion it was curious cows, which on closer inspection turned out to be bullocks and their copious 'cow-pats'.

Identity

Members of the group had cultural experience in their families where the presence of a crocodile in the river is an expected thing. Cultural perceptions, instincts, knowledge and impression of rivers affects our relationship and understanding of them. Putting a metaphorical crocodile into the river represented a dual cultural way of seeing. Not out of the ordinary in some participants' minds or memories, even a natural association for some, yet here in this Devon river valley most swimmers do not keep an eye out for crocodiles!

Main workshop aims

The previous weekend had been directed by the visual art input. This day was focused on storytelling. The featured story was a version of Cinderella mixed with another well-known storyline which suited the mixed-heritage group well. The main activity was the structured sharing of personal story anecdotes.

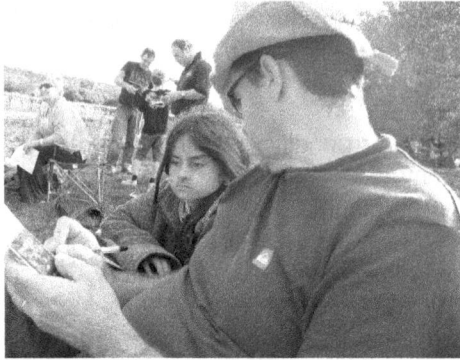

Story – workshop aims – Sara chose to:

- To invoke the story in the place.
- To encourage personal story sharing with a 'pocket size' memory activity.
- To encourage personal story sharing about people's favourite cultural food.

Visual art – workshop aims – Cara chose to:

- To create a piece of sculptural art from natural, and found, objects present at the site.
- To provide opportunities for drawing on a walk and encourage drawing skills.

Music – workshop aims – Hugh chose to:

- To learn an Indonesian song to sing as a group and complement the story.
- To write new songs.
- To display Asiatic gongs and bells, using them as part of a composition.

Cara seeded the idea of making a crocodile and then the design was up to those who chose to participate on that task. She provided a toolkit, advice where needed along with natural fibre string. Hugh chose to bring gongs, a xylophone, an Indonesian song and to use pebbles and sticks from the river bank to make music. The song Charisma the Crocodile was composed. This then became part of an avant-garde performance piece involving the whole group. Everyone walked from the river rubbing wet pebbles together, taking their place at the gongs and instruments for a sound-scape before singing the song. The walk was then reversed and ended with skimming our pebbles back into the water. It was light hearted, fun and expressive as well as quirkily musical.

The Penny Tree

To mark the end of the day, and the continuity of our journey, we took our pennies to a dead tree trunk and hammered them in with our wishes. A new penny tree was started.

Adult discussion group

As part of this workshop Parminder led a discussion group about parenting in a mixed-heritage family. This was scheduled after lunch while a parallel child friendly activity took place, allowing parents to talk privately about their experience without the children hearing. It solved the dilemma of some children recoiling at this topic of conversation while some parents were desperate to talk. Having other on-going activities supported the discussion group and provided a genuine alternative away from the conversation for those who did not want to participate. Parminder's observations are on page 87. The general discussion is in evaluation section on page 151.

Story synopsis:

The Crocodile's Tale.

A kind girl loses her cruel step-mother's golden sarong in the river as she washes it. A benevolent mother crocodile promises to find it if the girl looks after her baby. She looks after the baby crocodile so well that she is rewarded by dripping gold and jewels falling from her mouth when she speaks. The step-mother sends her own grumpy girl to repeat the process in the hope that she will meet the same fate. However she is mean to the baby crocodile and only mud and stones come from her lips when she speaks.

The chief's son is looking for a bride so he holds a party. The step-mother sends her grumpy daughter along and prevents the kind girl from attending because she has nothing fine to wear. The kind girl cries by the riverside, the crocodile appears and invites the girl to step inside her mouth. Full of fear she steps in and finds a beautiful, golden suit to put on. With a slap of the crocodile's tail she is transported to the party where she spends the whole night chatting to the prince. Dawn breaks; she rushes home and leaves a golden slipper behind. The prince promises to marry the girl whom the slipper belongs to. He eventually finds her; they marry and live happily ever after.

Our workshop was based on a story adapted by T. Robyn Batt from her book *The Fabrics of Fairytale*. (Batt. 2000)[1] and Jan Knappert's *Pacific Mythology* (Knappert 1992)[2]

Our crocodile

Sara Hurley's Tale
Story work

The Place.

I'm going to tell you about the day we spent on the river bank.

Lost is the wild, tumbling of the river's moorland descent, and the landscape is now one of broad meanders, rolling weirs, flood plains and ox-bow curves.

Flanking the river is a well-managed, pastoral landscape where cattle graze on lush, green grass beside river banks honeycombed with the nest holes of the pied flycatcher. The city is within walking distance.

We pitch up where the river is good for paddling by a pebbly beach and children can safely play.

The Idea

I wanted to bring in elements from other cultures to interact with the Devon landscape, just as the people brought their different cultural histories. I was interested in the group's conversation with the place and in listening to each other's personal stories.

The Story

As a starting point, I chose a story whose main characters were a benevolent crocodile and a young girl. I liked the story for a mixed-heritage group because it culturally represented a non-British way of life, yet its storyline paralleled two story types familiar to the group from their British side. Firstly, Cinderella and secondly, a well-known world story theme where a compassionate child is gifted with jewels falling from their mouth as they speak, and a selfish child who issues mud or slugs as they talk much to the disappointment of their expectant parents.

Once we had located a conducive place to hold the workshop and investigated the site ideas began to flow that brought the stories' mood, images and the place together. I began to think about the questions I would ask to invite the family groups to share their personal stories and anecdotes in a contained way, alongside how I would interpret and tell the story. The story had informed our thinking and its resonance would emerge in a holistic, experiential way throughout the day.

I perceived the day as symbolically mixed heritage. The sound vibrations of gongs displayed on an overhanging branch inter-mingled with the ringing from nearby church bells. The group placed the crocodile as though it had just crawled out of the water into the Devon landscape. We ate cultural food for our picnic: coconut and lentil dahl, Mexican wedding biscuits, fried plantain, Welsh brack cake.

Personal storytelling.

I asked people to bring three things with them. A family day out involves carrying much 'stuff' so these were - food excepted - deliberately small.

1. Food to share with a special memory and from a culture that you like.

2. An object from home that is special to you and can fit in your pocket.

3. A penny.

Finding the right question

I spend time thinking about the right question to ask. The question has to fit the people, place and workshop because it can direct the themes, flow and outcome enormously. Subtle choices have to be made. This workshop was nearly about 'lost and found' but it didn't feel right for a self-referring, occasional group with a broad age range. In this context these questions gave people room to choose how to present themselves without being intrusive into personal life, family history or dynamics. It is important that the question is always an open question and doesn't contain suggestions, choices or judgements.

The food question

I wanted the question/invitation to be open to bring any food regardless of the participant's culture(s). A person may not know much about their culinary heritage, a family may not want to present their special cultural dish like a party piece, or they may be proud to do so. A mixed-heritage child may have their own views on favourite cultural food and what they are willing to go public about. I wanted to leave the door wide open for dishes from a place that inspired individuals whatever the reason or connection.

Food

I recommend using food in a workshop whenever possible. It's a great thing to share; relationships deepen over food and it's a wonderful area to explore from many angles: origins, recipes, culture, traditional stories, family stories, habits and personal memories are all rich conversational possibilities. A shared meal quickly becomes a feast and 'breaking bread' together has the potential to aid creativity, increase well-being and strengthen relationships. For many people a shared meal is an opportunity to experiment and eat a variety of good food. Food was an important part of our time together because of the length of the sessions and the family orientation.

Shared lunch

We laid out our dishes on a table cloth that covered the part-grass, part-river beach ground where we sat. After taking in the smells and sights of the food, we introduced our dishes, and told our stories about them.

The array of foods whetted everyone's taste buds for travel; each dish spoke of places around the world brought to life through personal storytelling and descriptions of other landscapes where the food had been eaten, whether a Goan bay, a Welsh field, a Mexican city, a Gambian compound, a Norfolk kitchen or a Middle Eastern street.

The unexpected addition to this conversation was the idea of what people would have bought if they could, which took us into the limitless world of imagined dishes.

Sentences began, "I brought _____ but I could have brought_____."

This broadly covered two areas.

Firstly: the family who, for whatever reasons, didn't bring a 'special dish' but brought themselves, food to share and their stories. Sometimes this is all we can manage and it is enough just to get yourself and the family out of the house.

Secondly: we could talk about more complex favourite dishes and enter the delicious world of the imagination. Everyone could contribute through storytelling, conjuring wonderful dishes in our mind's eye without feeling lesser, or outside of the group.

Our tongues had acted as gateways to rich memories and special places. By the end of the meal, our senses were alive, our friendships strengthened and we were all the more relaxed and ready to play.

Memory question

Bringing an object from home imbued with a special memory felt like an amusing and practical rule to set. Finding a theme, or rule, can be helpful for people to know what to bring as well as opening up specific, and often more interesting, personal stories.

Pocket size memories

Before we shared our objects, it seemed that everyone had magical time capsules in their pockets; secrets ready to burst with flavour, gifts of story tucked just out of sight waiting to be unwrapped.

I used simple methods of pair and small-group talking to support sharing of personal stories. This approach usually puts people at ease as they're able to explore and rehearse their stories in a familiar, conversational style before they share and talk to the whole group. Practically this approach also allows more time to explore themes in the workshop.

Here's an outline of my questions which enable easy ways to get a group talking and listening within time limits along with my reasoning.

Turn to someone near you and find a partner.

This is a natural way of encouraging new conversations without always sticking with 'safe' friends or avoiding others. It helps to encourage quick choices.

In pairs decide who's A and B and take it in turn to talk about the object you have brought with you. Setting a time limit of 2-3 minutes is usually beneficial.

A talks about the object while B listens without interrupting.

The process is then reversed.

Storytelling is about talking and listening which are both skills that can be finely tuned. Timing how long each person speaks for gives a boundary which encourages respectful listening and where the talker knows they have uninterrupted space. Time limits balance the talkative with the less talkative, improving freedom of speech and focus.

The Baka tribe of Cameroon use singing as a leveller in their community; songs are sung with everyone contributing their part. Someone who sings too quietly or too dominantly is said to 'steal the song'. The same can be said for talking and listening where the story is stolen in the same way. It is useful to remember that the person who doesn't contribute much can steal the story just as much as the person who talks a lot.

Su Hart [1]

There is music for ritualistic purposes, music for passing on knowledge, stories and the history of the Baka people, and music for pure enjoyment. There is no sense of performer and audience. There will be leaders in the music, for example when a story is told in song, but all will join in with the choruses, or with harmonies and with percussion accompaniment. This communal music-making constantly helps to strengthen the bonds between the individuals in the groups.

Martin Cradick. [2]

Find another pair to join up with and make a group of four.

Each pair tells the other pair their story except now the A's tell the B's story and B's tell the A's story around the four.

Each individual's story begins its own life and the individual storyteller's memory engages. How does our story change, or sound, when it's told by someone else?

The experience lies in the telling, listening and sharing. Pair and small group work has a similar effect on the individual as telling a story to the whole group. The relaxed intimacy can foster developments or amplifications of the anecdote. Anxiety about talking to a group is reduced as the small group provides a safe rehearsal and validating audience for the story and the teller. It's a warm up so the teller isn't going in 'cold'.

Would anyone like to tell any of the stories they've heard to everybody?

Here is the opportunity to tell the whole group and, on the whole, most people are now relaxed enough to share. Sometimes a whole 'go round' is not a great use of time and slows potential follow on activities. In other workshops it is an essential part of equalising the group process, particularly for 'circle' or group time and democratic sharing. Introductory games like this encourage and prepare for improved talking and listening in the circle.

Working together and communicating in a circle is fundamental to people where like King Arthur's round table or a gathering around an outdoor fire. Circle Time has become accepted practice in many schools to develop the foundational skills of empathy, motivation, understanding and managing feelings, being able to get along with others. These skills are just as important as academic skills in explaining success. (Mosely and Sonnet 2006 [3])

Give out small pieces of paper. Write, draw, or both, about your object, the memory and what it means to you.

This activity contains the stories and allows the group to share further. The paper stories can be spread out, pinned up, used to decorate something and speak volumes about the group and its time.

Answers

One pair was desperate to share because they couldn't believe the co-incidence of them both pulling sea urchins from their pockets!

Each tiny personal anecdote is highly individualistic, full of feeling and personality. In group poem, story making and song writing, even a sentence or a few spoken words is a nugget of juicy information that can be put together with other people's and creatively developed. Participants are quickly involved in the creative process. They are listening and being listened to, acknowledged and acknowledging, regardless of age or 'ability', they are contributing to and helping develop the wider story.

A themed question or use of an object can help people to feel comfortable about talking and much can be safely shared and found. As a starter, it provides a tangible time, place or event to talk about. This is easier and safer as a way in than open questions about concepts or feelings. Bigger and more complex questions are intrinsically linked with the subject anyway and will emerge later if it is safe and appropriate to do so.

Initially an object or drawing can act as a prop to support the telling without the teller feeling self-conscious or it can act as a shield against embarrassment. In very confident or energetic people it can help define thoughts and contain them before it is time to move on to the next stage.

More quietly, we can take our memories out for an airing, dust them off, share them, take a fresh look and replace them a little bit renewed and feel all the better for it.

The purpose of using story based talking and listening activities in this workshop was to invite the group to share new things about themselves and strengthen group and family feeling. It had a social, expressive and performance function with the emphasis on developing relationships and a sense of community.

Bring a penny.

The day ended with a wish and a bash! In the fading, yellow light of evening the group ambled over the river beach, past the crocodile and the gongs hanging in the tree, to a small glade with a dead tree branch in it. Ritualistically we hammered our pennies into it and made a wish. A wish as individual and unique as our objects and food stories and the memories we had made that day. The penny tree is still there for other people to add their own wishes to, like a marker in our story map of the river.

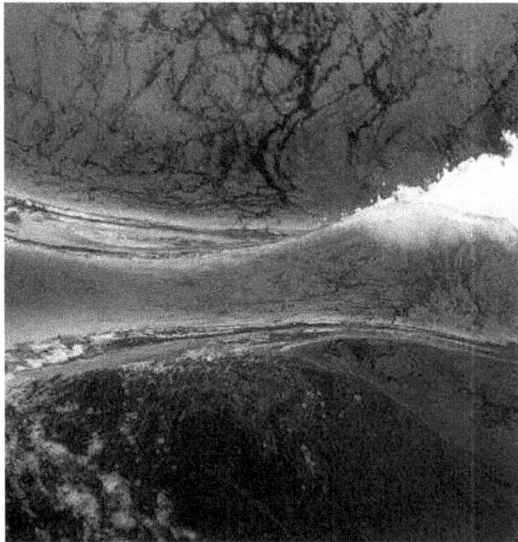

Parminder Southcott's Tale
Mixed-heritage family work

Introduction

My background is in community work, offering support and guidance to families and professionals about understanding mixed heritage identity, parenting mixed heritage children and cross cultural communication within a rural and urban context. I have provided group sessions where families, children and young people can come together with others like themselves to explore their individual mixed identities and begin to understand how this influences their roles within their family system. My overall aim has been to promote positive mental health and emotional wellbeing for those who identify and feel a sense of belonging to this group of mixed heritage people.

I'd like to tell you a bit about my background and how I came into this work. I'm from mixed Indian parentage and was trans-racially adopted into a white family as a baby. I grew up in Exeter in the 70's, unsure of who I was, with limited contact and relationships with my Indian family. I later married, had mixed-race children and continued to live in Exeter.

In 2002 I started The Planet Rainbow Project in Exeter with Kayte Price after an incident within my own family which clarified the lack of support, provision or recognition, for the specific issues of being in a mixed race family. I looked for support and found nothing. There were no groups or agencies available in the community for black and ethnic minority families and, at that time, mixed-race was identified as belonging to this group.

In 2001 I had the idea to provide a support service for families who identified themselves as being mixed-race or mixed-heritage. A local family centre was incredibly supportive and for two years Kayte and I worked voluntarily while we gathered evidence of need so we could access funding. We began with a coffee morning and a questionnaire; within 10 minutes 12 families walked through the door and from then on we didn't look back.

In 2004 The Planet Rainbow Project began with two workers providing regular family activities, building relationships with other organisations and generally raising awareness about mixed-race issues. We were persistent, sometimes troublesome, in our efforts to raise awareness within social, racial and community organisations. Previously, mixed-race-ness was not seen as having a separate identity to other racial groups. The similarities were evident, in terms of skin colour and racism yet with distinct differences.

To example frequently experienced specific issues:

Indirect racism and discrimination can come from both sides of the family. Not being totally with one culture or another is stressful; not looking like your parents can be socially and emotionally awkward; finding people 'like us' and chatting or playing naturally can be hard to come by.

Single white parents can feel isolated or inferior which undermines feelings of confidence and competence in their parenting. Often this is experienced around hair and skin care issues where people feel particularly vulnerable to criticism.

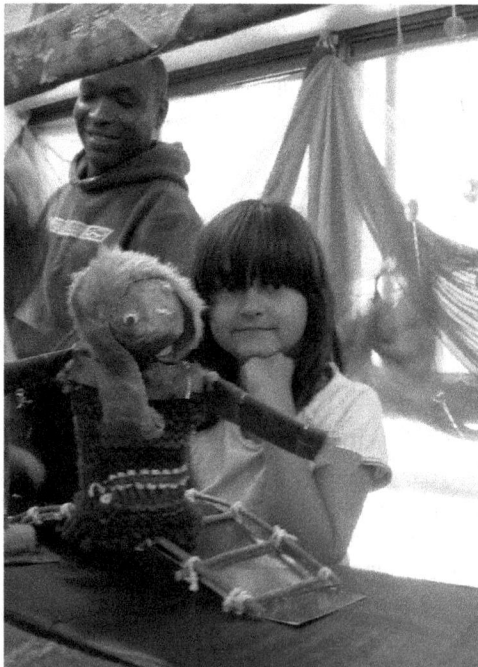

The 'Tail to Tale' project

It is normal for children and young people to have an overarching desire to fit in. Being confused about their identity complicates this. This desire to fit in can often result in very uncomfortable feelings of wanting to be white because it is the prevailing culture. In extreme cases an internalised racism can take hold.

Parents from different racial backgrounds can empathise hugely with their child/ren, but they can never fully know their experience of being mixed.

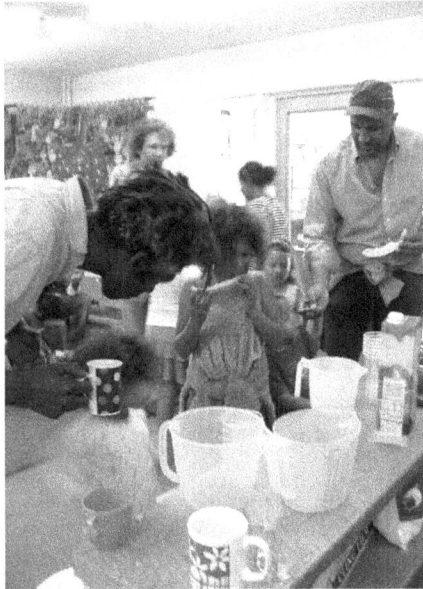

In 2007 The Planet Rainbow Project began to partner with Blazing Tales. Sara a storyteller/ community artist with mixed-race/ mixed-heritage children approached me as she was interested in working on a creative project with other mixed families. Funding was secured for the 'Tail to Tale' project thanks to Awards for All, National Lottery.

I saw this as an excellent way to bring the families together to work collectively, providing opportunities for them to explore their identities through participation and conversation with each other. As there was a pre-dominance of white single-mums the sessions provided opportunities for children with absent fathers, or limited contact, to work alongside Dads from other cultures who could be role models. Working with the puppets, song writing and world stories drew out real life situations. Confidences were strengthened through the chance to make something as well as developing new friendships and connections.

Families who identified themselves as being mixed-race or mixed-heritage were themselves hugely varied. For some the children were obviously mixed and brown skinned, for other children their mixed-ness was less externally visible, or a parent was mixed and the child looked white. The Planet Rainbow Project also welcomed step-families with mixed members. One of the roles of the organisation was to offer support to families who were trans-racially adopting and we offered support to the first same-sex trans-racial adoption in Devon.

The Planet Rainbow Project sadly closed in 2009 due to lack of funding. We had had a fluid membership of 65 families from Devon with a core group of around 10 families who regularly attended monthly activities.

My role was as a freelance family support worker on the 'river exe-pedition', and many families who had been members of The Planet Rainbow Project attended.

My role involved:

- Liaising between the artists and the families, the role had a mediating quality, translating between different approaches and understandings.

- Encouraging a culture of conversation around mixed-heritage issues both formally and informally.

- To be supportive to any family member raising identity issues. To decide when this should be recorded or reported.

- To be a point of contact for family members.

- To give practical advice to family members about organisations and opportunities available to them.

It was part of my role to build trust and relationships with the children and young people. As I wasn't leading activities I was able to observe the children and chat with them during activities and they often talked to me about 'things' connected to their identity and families. There was a wide range of confidence in identity and self-esteem amongst them; their comfort in their own skin notably reflecting behaviour, attitude and choices. Having repeated contact meant that I could observe subtle changes and build on previous observation and conversations. Some children who had been initially defensive and confused grew relaxed and self-expressive, they showed more of their positive nature as the time went by.

The project: mixed-race and mixed heritage:

At the time of the project the name 'mixed-heritage' was largely in use. This had been influenced by The Planet Rainbow Project who had preferred this term due to the wide spectrum of member families. From my observations the naming was led by the parents and the children followed suit in how they referred to themselves. Despite this I now prefer to say mixed-race as it's less clumsy.

We all have different aspects to ourselves and part of growing up is learning how to move between these different aspects. However this normal process is greatly amplified for the mixed-race child and opportunities such as the 'river exe-pedition' allows for real practice in shifts in social inter-action, changes in subtle dynamics between different family members and friends, adults and children. With concentrated practice we become more comfortable with our different aspects, different selves, and with fluidity about the transitions the movement can be made with increased ease. Whilst parents can often empathise with their child's experience, it is the child's experience of their own mixed-ness right here, right now which has to be individually negotiated. A project like this allows exploration of these constant, subtle shifts in a supportive environment.

The process

The children especially appreciated having access to safe, open spaces away from their parents. They got just as much from the creative activities as they did the free play, although the activities helped them re-

91

focus. One break-away group were encouraged to participate when they were offered cameras to make films and take photos with. This also gave them a feeling of control and brought them back in with the group.

Hugh's method of song writing involves a lot of positive attention where children are heard and listened to. They can see something being made from their thoughts and ideas which is visibly and immediately empowering. I observed 100% engagement with the children and parents during the music workshops.

I also observed the parents discovering new or latent skills as they engaged with the other activities. In terms of informal discussion the parents made their own self-help group. At the first camp the parents were bursting to be able to talk to other parents and I was able to be involved in these conversations and encourage the informal culture of talking freely. Talking with others within an experience was a huge relief for many parents. They didn't have to explain themselves, or their child's colour, or deal with intrusive curiosity. Nor manage their own defensive reactions which their child could pick up on. Here they could be themselves and talk about it 'normally' without it being notable or different; the children played and created in the wide open spaces. The parents shared stories and incidences both positive and negative, they talked about the subtleties of mixed-heritage parenting and I saw them shine during an empowering, memorable time. The conversations were typical of any parenting conversation with the mixed issue being an extra dimension of care and consideration.

Over sewing or supper the parents also had time to reflect on how they were brought up and what their families were like. Sharing experiences and talking about what they had taken and what they had left behind from their upbringing, school and social experiences. Creating a community over the weekend meant that conversations could be dropped and later continued (like the sewing) and, as one mum said, it's amazing the bonds that can be made in just a few days, which was true for her and her child.

As I was 'on the ground' with the families and not a session leader I was challenged at times by group dynamics and different parenting styles. For example some parents welcomed other adults keeping an eye out for their child and disciplining where necessary, others not so much; at times I was quietly negotiating the micro-cultures of each family as the children naturally pushed boundaries and busily made their own groups and community.

Observations:

At times I experienced areas of conflict within me, frustration really. Being attuned I could see that there were issues of identity that required more in-put than the project could offer, or was about. At that time I had no way of communicating effectively with other professional organisations and I still had a desire to do more. I knew the project would end and realised the good work we could do to support the children and young people. I also knew that the specific support required would no longer be available for them to explore their identity as being mixed-heritage in Devon. I was aware that with the Planet Rainbow Project ending this issue was no longer being driven forward with other agencies about the specific needs of mixed-heritage families, or children and young people.

Appropriate supervision for this kind of work is an issue. I could seek supervision from professionals in social or racial work, but I knew of no mixed-race person in a high performing position to be able to offer me the supervision I felt I needed. New ventures always involve going into the unknown and the unknown always has elements which are surprising or unplanned.

Being involved in this project enabled me to broaden my professional experience of the familiar, indoor, more formal setting in children's centres to an outdoor, creative project where exploration was embraced and freedom encouraged. I had to get used to health and safety guidelines in an outdoor setting.

My previous experience had been as a session worker who provided activities, or offered family support in small numbers within walls. Initially I was out of my comfort zone trying to make personal sense of my role within the team on a new project never attempted before. I didn't want to come across as just a nosy session worker! My role seemed to fall between facilitation and support and I found it hard to organise it in my head. It was a big difference for me going from a half days sessional activity to living with people in a camp situation. It was a positive challenge and I liked having time to observe, talk, build relationships, learn and find my feet in a new way.

Midway through the project, in the lower Exe valley on the crocodile day, I felt that I finally started to build healthy and trusting relationships with the families and fully found my position within the team. This was well reflected in my performance on that day and from then on. I decided to 'back off' a bit. In fact in my backing off and changing my perception of what it meant to be a 'support worker' I became more relaxed and confident. I saw my supportive role as facilitating conversations and connecting with people through the activities.

Now I knew the participants, particularly the children, and I had established trust I could more effectively and personally engage with them. I gave plenty of positive strokes to individuals that lead into reflective conversations, and had some rich philosophical chats. The wreath making on the final day at Exmouth encouraged these philosophical chats. As the group discussed the recipe for Peace, splinter groups of children and adults picked up on the themes and ran with them. The project was coming to a close.

As a new project I tried to be fluid in my role and as it evolved I gained great insight into how to be in this situation. On a personal note I was disappointed that the Planet Rainbow Project had come to an end, seeing opportunities to engage with families and develop awareness which I was now unable to do. My hopes were low. I thoroughly enjoyed the experience and gained great insight into my personal and professional development. It was a meaningful time for the families who really appreciated spending time together with the added adventure of exploring Devon along the River Exe and creatively making their presence known in the county.

Parminder Southcott's Tale was written by Sara from notes written by Parminder and conversations with Parminder.

Exeter

'Wells and Walls'

Looking around you.

I feel it is so important my daughter feels she has a connectedness with Devon as well as the connections with Jamaica, Nigeria and London.

Locations

The Exeter day was the urban experience of the 'river exe-pedition' with distinct workshops taking place at different venues. The families could pick and mix the workshops or come for the whole day. Other Exeter organisations and people were involved in the preparation and delivery of this event: The Spacex Gallery, Crab Man - Phil Smith, the Royal Albert Memorial Museum (RAMM) at St. Nicholas' Priory made significant contributions.

The morning was hosted by The Spacex Contemporary Art Gallery where the group visited an exhibition and Blazing Tales led a workshop in response. After lunch the group either left, or visited the medieval St. Nicholas Priory which was refurbished in Tudor times as a grand town house. After a workshop there on River Trade led by the education officer, the group gathered for a Mis-guided tour with mythogeographer Phil Smith - aka the Crab Man. The walk left the priory and wove its way to Exeter's historic quay, where everyone enjoyed some refreshment in a café. Blazing Tales closed the day.

Some history:

The history of The Exe informed the day's activities more directly than on previous events. It was an invitation for the group to learn and experience how Exeter had taken part in global history and trade.

Phil crying for a pastoral Exeter that never was.

The photo above shows Phil Smith telling us how Exeter was once as important and large a port as Manchester. He placed onions beneath his eyes to make him cry for the lost, nostalgic days when Exeter was a modest city served by and serving small local farms and supporting the wool industry. He suggests that this was never really the case. Wool played its part, but Exeter has been so much more than the provincial county town it is portrayed to be, directly because of the River Exe.

During the walk Phil told us about riots, epidemics and folk history along with the constant movement and friction between different religious and ethnic groups; within Christianity, between the Celts and other local factions. We were once again reminded how the world's water ways connect people and heard about marginalised people and forgotten facts. He took us to the Roman wall, parts of which still stand, and showed us volcanic bricks marked with evidence of river activity from the city sites pre-historic past.

How that connects globally:

The Exe from Exeter down to Topsham and Exmouth has a fascinating history linking it to the rest of the world over time. Feuds over land rights, poor navigability and the power of the Courtenay family were instrumental in the making of the Exeter Canal. We learnt a lot of real history on this day, not just a sugared, received wisdom, touristic version of events.

Blazing Tales creative response to this location.

How the place affected our creative decisions:

Our aim was to make the day personal for the group, we were keen that it should not simply be an historical day out that might feel interesting, but removed. We wanted to match the general global history with the small and personal to enhance meaning and make connections. As much as the knowledge received during the day supported their personal sense of self in the world, we sought to bring it in even closer and link with thinking about identity.

Blazing Tales workshop – Identity Cards.

As Sara wrote in her journal: *Identity - another over used, multi-interpretational buzz word, we can try and make our own sense of it on this day.*

As we mulled over ideas Cara, who loves puns, said "What about Identity Cards?" We took this idea - with a twist of course! These would be personal documents, like a bank card, that would reflect the personality and stories of individuals. Each artist led a short in-put using their own art form to elicit a unique personal out-put. (How we made the identity cards and what they looked like is shown in the accompanying book.)

Exhibition visit

Shaun Gladwell is an Australian artist who, critically and poetically links personal experience with contemporary culture and historical references. His works engage these concerns through forms of urban expression. (Gladwell. 2009)[1]

The themes of personal experience, contemporary culture and historical references in Gladwell's work touched on the emphasis of our day. We liked the fact that he expressed these themes through forms of urban expression. This naturally appealed to the young people in the group who could sometimes be caught between what they perceived to be activities for younger children and interested parents.

At Shaun Gladwell film exhibition at The Spacex Gallery

We loosely attempted to reference Gladwell's input during the day. It altered our perceptions and put a new slant on the frolics and movements of the children on the walk through the urban landscape. The following photos were taken by the 10-14 year olds on Blackberry phones.

KEEP CLEAR

River Trade Workshop at St. Nicholas Priory

This workshop had different activities that could be dipped in and out of.

- Dressing up in Tudor Clothes: The building was first built for a relative of William the Conqueror although it was later renovated and at its heyday in Tudor times. It has since been authentically restored to its former Tudor glory and welcomes visitors for an interactive Tudor experience including a range of period clothing.

- Making swan boats: The nearby Topsham Museum features a collection of unique and historic Exe river craft including the delightfully eccentric Cygnet boat which was originally a tender to a larger 'Swan', a mahogany skiff.

- A magnetic fishing game with the types of fish to be found in The Exe, notably salmon.

- A board style treasure hunt action game about global trade from the Exe that involved the buying and selling of wool, spice, slaves and potatoes. A group of parents and children enjoyed dressing up and acting out. A passionate discussion about the slave trade was stimulated by this activity which was informative for the children and made comprehensible through the game.

Young person dressing up in period clothes

Parent dressing up in period clothes

Mythogeographer, Phil filled us full with history, anecdote, image, story and his personal overlaying of ideas and information threaded it all together. His walk took us on a tour of Exeter's water ways: wells, pipes, St. Sidwella, the Carrefour, Cricklepit Mill and the quay. He told us how cholera had affected the city, and likened the invading cholera antibodies to the comings and goings of tribes and people throughout history.

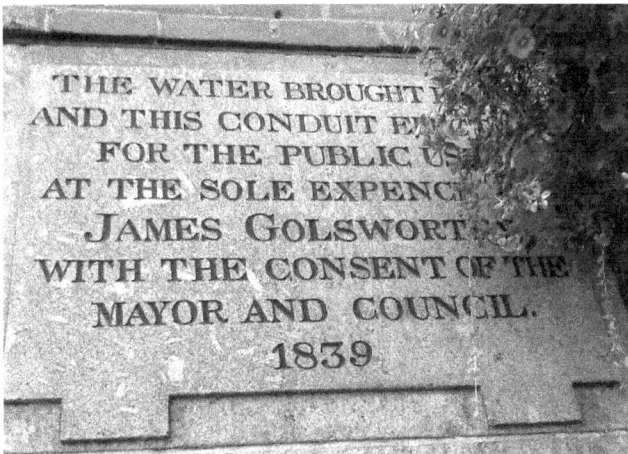
Memorial

Exploring the water conduit

Matthew the Miller clock on St. Mary Steps Church

Phil told us how folk history says the people of Exeter kept their time by the punctuality of Matthew the Miller. This story was thought to be quaint hearsay until documentary evidence later proved it to be true.

Tea, Story and Evaluation Forms.

It was a busy day with people able to drop in and out of the workshops on offer. After it all a drink, some cake, a nice sit down and a story was needed. We went to a quay side café situated inside one of the old storage cellars where the BBC filmed 'The Onedin Line' in the 1970's.

Story synopsis

King Solomon's Ring.

King Solomon gives his servant what he thinks is an impossible task. He sends him to go in search of a ring that will make a sad person happy and a happy person sad. After many adventures and much travelling around the globe, the servant returns to the same market place where he started and prepares to tell King Solomon the bad news that he cannot find such a ring. As he searches the market place below the castle in a final attempt to complete his task he meets an old trader who unexpectedly solves his problem. The trader engraves the words: 'This too shall pass' onto an old lead ring and gives it to the servant.

In response to his quest the servant passes the ring on to King Solomon. Solomon, famous for being the wealthiest King in all history, looks around his golden palace at his incredible riches and feels sad that 'this too shall pass'. The poor, weary servant with no place to sleep that night also feels happy in the knowledge that 'this too shall pass'. Here is the ring that will make the sad person happy and the happy person sad. For nothing stays the same.

Our workshop was based on the story King Solomon's Ring adapted from a traditional Jewish tale. This version is from 'Telling Tales' by Taffy Thomas and Steve Killick. (2007)[2]

Phil Smith's Tale
Mis-Guided Tours

How to make a Mis-Guided Tour

A mis-guided tour is a performance modelled on the conventional guided tour, but one in which the role and tactics of the conventional tour guide are fore-grounded - made explicit and obvious. The usual historical mono-narrative or jumble of factual snippets in a general wash of "history", is replaced by a series of layers and tangents, with enough connections to allow the tour's audience to begin to make their own meanings from the route.

A 'mis-guide' should have fun with the authoritative voice of the conventional guide, highlighting their role by comic imitation of a guide's dress and props: blazer, folder, etc. Or, paradoxically, the guide should overtly deny such expectations. Dispensing with the conventional reserve of the guide, the 'mis-guide' should be immersed in their tour. On my Exe-pedition tour I gave the audience cups of water to throw over me, re-enacting an old privilege of the residents on our route.

The layers of subject matter should be various: autobiographical, at moments intensely materialist in an attention given to extreme detail: of the chemistry or morphology of building materials, for example. Or critical: challenging assumptions or conventional narratives about the tour's route. The mis-guide should draw equally on respectable and unrespectable knowledges: on the physics of geology, on the stories of hauntings. The connectedness of the tour is achieved by rearranging established narratives to reveal ironical and unexpected connections, by researching and revealing hidden histories, and by introducing the guide's own responses and associations to the places or themes of the tour. 'Mis-guides' reveal themselves as subjective and compromised voices, part of the meaning-making of these places, implicitly criticising the traditional apparent 'objectivity' of the conventional guide.

So, to make a 'mis-guided tour', find a route or a defined site. Research that site for: official documentation and for marginalised or ignored data; unreliable stories and gossip; accounts of anomalies; previous performances in the site; previous uses; mundane stories about the place; crass statistics and sublime physical information – vulcanology, for example. Then research the site physically: climb on it, crawl over it, hide in it, eat in its cafes, wash in its showers, talk to everyone in it, sample its textures and tickle up your own autobiographical associations. This should reveal various layers of meaning, which then are assembled and connected in a way which allows new, hybrid meanings to occur to an audience. The most evocative way of allowing audiences to make connections is to show something early on that appears to be a tangent, a humorous curiosity, but is later 'folded back' into the tour to reveal a deeper and different significance.

The most important thing that a 'mis-guided tour' can produce is a hyper-sensitised audience. To enable this, the audience should find themselves co-opted into the performance: physically modelling events, holding objects, touching surfaces, tasting and drinking.

Mythogeography

Mis-guided tours are one aspect of a part serious, part comical practice called "mythogeography" that sprang from the work of site-specific artists Wrights & Sites. The group became increasingly aware of pressures that generated monolithic and restrictive tellings about some of the sites in which they were working – particularly touristic and heritage spaces. As the strategies and tactics deployed to loosen up these restrained meanings accumulated, the group called this "mythogeography".

So, "mythogeography" is a philosophy, an emerging strategy and a growing set of tactics for exploring and celebrating the multiplicitous nature of places. It expresses the nature of space itself, which by its unfinishedness and its under-constructedness always tends to resist attempts to restrict its meanings. In this sense, "mythogeography" helps along certain opportunities in its sites.

Leats and Arrivals

For the 'river exe-pedition' I researched and led a mis-guided tour, the kind of guided tour that trips over its own feet, based on some of the features of those parts of Exeter that the Blazing Tales journeyers were passing through.

As I explored the route in preparation, from The Mint to the Quay I perused some research notes and newspaper clippings about the area. What struck me first were the boundaries of the city walls: the walk touched the North wall and passed through its Southern stretch. Then there were the transitory qualities: the West Quarter and the Quay with their flows of water, people, cargoes, capital, sewerage and ideas. Finally, there were ideas about other, different kinds of arrivals and impacts. I wondered how to set each of these ideas in motion in relation to others. In the end, for most of that work, I could let the audience do themselves.

The city walls are boundaries built by Roman colonists which have been rebuilt many times. They are pierced or levelled in numerous places, and they are in motion, eroding records of extreme climates: bubbled rocks from volcanic eruptions and breccias from windswept Permian deserts.

Then there are the individual stories: Father Oliver, for example, the early nineteenth century Catholic priest whose public service, particularly during times of cholera, transformed the image of immigrant Catholics in what could quickly become a rioting, protesting, militantly Protestant city. Or the groups: some transitory and exotic like the stripy-jumpered Onion Johnnies selling strings of onions door to door; others such as the Dutch merchants or the refugees from the Irish famine who came and stayed.

All this took place in sites that were ambiguous and unstable: waters that were both polluted and clean, safe one year and deadly the next. There were man-made leats – small streams- which powered the mills and mills that rotted, one being rebuilt as a spectacle of itself. Although I didn't know it until we were approaching it, the fulcrum of this mis-guided tour was to be a maze inside the grounds of that renovated mill. But, when we got there, the gates were locked. It was almost better that way: to be forced to describe the motion of walking a maze, and the effect it has on the liquids of the brain. To imagine from outside it, to be dis-placed at the moment that should have been most embodied, most sited, most inward and intimate.

Further information on mythogeography is available in 'Mythogeography: a guide to walking sideways'. (Smith. 2010)[1]

Exmouth

'Garlands and Waves'

Timing and flow

I loved the boat ride and conversations. I've forged a link with some of these places.

Location

Exmouth is at the end of the river where it opens to the sea. A sea-side town on the estuary.

This last day had a poignancy that was echoed in the geography around us: endings and beginnings, direction and dissolution all reflecting the cyclical nature of life.

The group met on the dock for a boat trip on the last of the 11am to 5pm days. A Caribbean lunch was cooked by a local family then delivered to a 1940's built council hall opposite the sea front. It was now November, the clocks had gone back and the nights were drawing in. Our day was short, and as the evening light came quickly in, the group spent time on the beach where we ended our journey with songs, garlands, paddling, frolicking, messages and thanks.

Some history

The Exmouth visit took place over the November Remembrance weekend. As I read the words on Exmouth's war memorial I was put in mind of earlier tragedies of unnamed people from other lands who had lost their lives on Devon's shores, alongside those brave men and women killed during the atrocities of more recent wars.

Decades of easy peace may go their way
And tide and time may drift us far apart
But you who shared our savage yesterday
Will hold the highest places in our heart.

Words on Exmouth's war memorial

Along with: *is it nothing to all ye who pass by? We will remember them.*

It was pertinent for our group at the end of their journey to remember people from other countries and continents who had arrived or left from here or who had fallen at sea. As this was the last event we had also created our own history, story, memories and had each other to thank and remember.

How does this connect globally?

Exmouth has a long maritime history and is still a working dock.

It is self-evident that Devon has not the history of slavery and black immigration that some parts of the country have had. The comparative lack of references in financial papers indicates the local economy was never built on slavery, a supposition confirmed by published histories of the sixteenth to eighteenth centuries. Individual merchants and gentlemen had estate interests in the West Indies but to a lesser degree than in Ireland.

Gray. 1999[1]

On the boat journey we passed Powderham Castle, home of the once globally and nationally powerful Courtenay Family, whose wealth and estates reached around the world; notably with sugar trade to the West Indies.

Blazing Tales creative response

Workshops

- Boat trip
- Caribbean lunch
- Two stories

- Choice: music workshop, visual arts workshop, young people's discussion
- Closing on the beach

Boat Trip

The artists had planned to ask people to design and write a postcard to someone else on the boat about something that they'd liked on the exepedition, or at least to draw on the cards about a moment they'd shared. We also wanted to talk to people and find words and ideas for songs and poems.

In actuality it wasn't possible for two main reasons. Firstly, there was a constant tour guide tape playing. Secondly, everyone was so pleased to see each other again, talk, play and experience the boat trip, take turns steering the boat and explore that it felt valuable to let the natural momentum of the day and personal experience have it's time. The group cohesion felt more important than us forcing our 'things to do' upon them.

Cara did some drawing with some younger children, Hugh and Sara talked to people and Tony filmed, including a full rainbow in the sky.

The boat

Sara wrote in her journal:

The boat trip was a wonderful way to start the day. The weather was once again totally glorious for us. After a rainy start the clouds were soon whisked away on the November breeze, exposing a high blue sky, moody grey around the edges; a day when you can really delight in the unpredictable, ever changing British weather.

We had hoped to write a song on the boat, but as it turned out it was a fantastic way for everyone to catch up with each other informally. Friends old and new, and many new bonds between children, parents, families have been made, and between us –the artists- and with all of them too. We have seen some of these children grow up and develop in the time we've been working with them. The project has continued as lots has changed in some people's lives.........much more ease between people, children settled where there was some tension early on.

Story synopsis:

Death in a Nut.

Jack's mother is on her death bed. In a state of confusion and upset Jack goes for a walk along the beach where he meets Death who happens to be strolling along the sea shore on his way to visit Jack's mum. Jack tries to stop him, they argue and Jack manages to outwit Death by beating him with his scythe until he is small and then trapping him in a nut and throwing him far out to sea. He soon realises that life is impossible when nothing dies. He can't crack an egg for his breakfast or have a slice of bacon, he can't cut wood or put out fires. He eventually finds the nut washed up on the shore, releases Death and everything returns to normal. Jack's mother has a wise word with him. She says everyone has a time to be born and a time to die. She accuses Jack of stealing her moment from her. Eventually she is able to welcome her release from pain and suffering and die. In his grief he accepts the cycle of life and death. (Williamson 1989)[2]

Yemanja, Queen of The Sea.

Traditional Yoruba Myth and Brazilian Story.

Yemanja is the daughter of the Goddess Olokun, goddess of the waters. She marries a powerful king and has lots of children. Stifled by palace life and goes to her mother for help. Olokun gives her a pot of charmed water. Yemanja breaks the pot in two and the charmed water carries her out to sea where she finds her freedom. She begins a new life beneath the waves with her musician. As Queen of the Sea she links West Africa with Brazil and is still celebrated in both places today where she is gifted with flowers and necklaces.

Music Workshop

Our version of the Yemanja story flows seamlessly into a Samba workshop as we chant words from the story in syncopating samba rhythms. The group split and some adults went to write a new song with Hugh. Read Hugh's tale for a full account of his approach to song writing.

Choosing flowers

Visual art

Cara led the activity to make a large wreath from fresh flowers to give to the sea at the end of the day. This collective piece of art making was made from natural materials to be left in the place after we had gone. This activity both echoed the poppy wreaths that were to be laid across Britain the following day and also the flowers that are traditionally given to the sea as part of honouring the sea goddess in Brazil.

The garland in progress

Story making

As the group wove the garland Sara got them talking about their recipe for a better world, one that has learnt to improve from a past of war and brutality. A collective poem was written in the form a recipe as a group of around eight related and unrelated adults, children and young people discussed the qualities and ideas they'd like to see more of in the world. Others chipped in from around the circle and through scribing and decision making a collective piece was made. Two young people pulled the whole thing together and took ownership of the next stage when we put this message in a bottle. It was sealed and given to the sea complete with date, context and contact details (not strictly an environmentally friendly thing to do but romanticism won the day!)

Writing a group poem

Young people's talk time

This was offered to the group but there was a unanimous feeling that they preferred to be creative at that point. With the shortening days this day had enough going on in it and limited space to contain the conversation. Was the relaxed feeling that both parents and children were happy doing what they were doing and hanging out together a positive culmination of our approach? The early intensity around the burning, sometimes prickly, issue of mixed-ness in Devon was now transformed. Bonds and relationships had been found, strengthened and settled into. Our early decision to take a largely organic approach to the issue was now working. One that on the whole did not impose 'talking about it' but let it rise to the surface in multiplicitous small and personal ways.

To the sea

In the dimming light everybody left the hall in a ramshackle procession carrying the wreath, singing as much of the song as anyone knew it by then, and crossed the zebra crossing, (Abbey Road, Beatle's style), to the beach.

In the wind we huddled and sang and tried to put the wreath in the sea, helped most by one woman who bravely whipped off her trousers and dragged it into the foam. To more song and cheer the bottle was thrown in. Music was played, by Hugh and a parent on her violin, and then we returned back over the zebra crossing to the hall to say our goodbyes to each other.

Footprints in the sand

Hugh Nankivell's Tale
The Source and the Mouth Of Songs

The life of songs

When we make songs we don't know what their life will be. We can't predict whether they will be popular and sell thousands of copies or whether they will never be sung again after the makers leave the room where they were made. But, for me, the important thing is being in that creative moment and actually being part of a collective that makes something. A group that has a shared experience of creating a song together about a shared activity or experience (or individual experiences, but on the same subject) is a really powerful thing.

Beginnings and baggage

Wherever I go I have baggage attached. When I arrived at Exford youth hostel on a grey February Friday evening I came with a set of hand chimes and some percussion instruments, a guitar, some large sheets of paper and some ideas. I also came with my history as a musician, father, teacher and songwriter. I arrived at a place I had been to once before. It had echoes of a long day walking on Exmoor and a blazing row with one of my sons counterbalanced with the peace and quiet of the National Park. More positives than negatives. But still I arrived with a 'not-knowing' question mark. I drove with Ellen, my daughter, through the misty moor. Both of us excited. We knew there would be friends there when we arrived: Sara, Parminder and Cara, but also a lot of new people we hadn't met before. Would they get on with us, would they bond with each other, would our programme of ideas, be acceptable, would they like the food, would they moan and not be able to sleep in the youth hostel dorms and beds? All of these things travelled through my mind as I arrived to meet a new group on a new project.

So I came with a menu of options. I had written down a series of games that we could play as icebreakers and as bonders and a set of songs that I could sing to the group and a few ideas for creating something new. My history and philosophy is (nearly) always to do something new. I don't have a repertoire of standards or pop songs or end-of-the-pier stories. I have me and what I can make and a short repertoire of songs that I have made with other people. Two or three of these get used regularly - for instance 'All the Animals of the Sea' a song I wrote with a group of kids from a youth centre in the West End of Newcastle about 20 years ago. It's a great collective song and also it is a song that demonstrates how verse/chorus songs might be put together. So on a song-writing project I often sing this song as a listening, a relaxing and an educational exercise.

Gradually people arrived in the dusk on the moor of The Exe near to the source of the river.

First song

In the evening I got started with making a song. I had a mix of people, young and old, some clearly comfortable, some apparently uncomfortable. I had a guitar. We made a song called 'Another World'. I asked the group to tell me things that happened to them on the way to Exford, and what they felt like when they arrived. We had a line or a word from everyone in the room. They all 'invented' their idea. I then set about helping them to 'arrange' those ideas into some sort of a shape, a pattern. We found some rhymes, we put a group of phrases together, without thinking long and hard about it. In fact it is all a bit jumbled up - line 1 is about 'here' the place, lines 2 and 3 about the journey to the place and line four again about 'here'... but we didn't worry about this.

Another World

Verse 1

It's like another world here

Didn't really know where I was going

I got lost on the way here

But now I'm here I feel like staying

Chorus

It's great here I think

Footloose and fancy free

Nothing and no-one's gonna bother me

As an icebreaking song-writing exercise it got us going and we made a song that everyone wanted to sing. I asked the group to come up with ideas for a melody when we had 2 verses and a chorus of words written up on a big sheet of paper. Lots of ideas came up, simple and catchy and I caught hold of them and framed them and added some chords and altered some rhythms, to help it fit. We started singing it very quickly and some people didn't stop singing it for much of the weekend.

Verse 2

My sister was really scared of the dark

I cuddled my lamby

And then my Mum felt sick

But now I'm here - I feel happy

Verse 3

We ate some yummy starbursts

We nearly missed our turning

Passing snowdrops on the way

But now I'm here - I'm opening the door

'Another World' does have a really catchy tune, and definitely worked for the group as a ground-breaking first 'exe-pedition' song, but even as it was being written I suspected that it may not have much longevity. I think the main reason for this is in the balance of the song's lyrics as a whole. Verse 1 and the chorus are fairly generic and could work for many types of song, but then suddenly in verse 2 and 3, it becomes a children's song. The grit of a personal statement that can become a pearl of a lyric in an individually composed song is much more difficult to manage within a collective song. First songs are often quirky songs, as the group finds a way to work together, and this was no exception.

In the collective song the workshop leader has to make decisions about how to shape the lines and melodies that s/he is offered and also what is most appropriate for that group at that particular time. So I was aware that as we were creating this song it might be that it was a song for that weekend and that weekend only. It served its purpose, getting us together to create, to understand how we could work and be with each other and was only the very beginning of our journey together.

A diversion

On a year-long large-scale community project in Sunderland, we needed a song to encapsulate 'Sunderland' the town, its history and a song which asked a question about the future, if possible. I knew this was a challenge and had tried to work on this with different choirs, community groups and schools. Each time we tried, something was not quite right, and usually a bit corny, something that was too specific or too generic, it wasn't quite there. Then one evening I had a young people's workshop between 6.30pm and 9.00pm. At the last minute it was cancelled (I forget why) but I still went along in case someone had not got the message. Two lassies arrived (aged about 10 or 11 - upper primary) and they said their Mam had left them there and gone out and would not be back till 9.00pm! So we had to have the workshop anyway! That evening the three of us created a wonderful song together. It was only six lines long, but encapsulated Sunderland. It was a song created by two local girls and me, a musician. Later we excitedly sang it to another colleague who loved it and later that summer it was sung by 450 people on stage outdoors at Hylton Castle. I write this to say that you can never predict what will happen at any workshop, but also that you cannot tell when you might get what you are looking for. It can come at any time, you just have to make sure that you are always looking.

Last song

The last song we wrote was at the mouth of The Exe at Exmouth, in early autumn. That day, before we wrote the final song, we had been on an estuary boat trip, eaten together and played some music together - a kind of rough and tumble samba for all thirty of us, led by me. We then divided into two groups, one (adults and children) to make a wreath of flowers to send out to sea and the other (adults only) to make a commemorative song to accompany this ceremony. So really it was a theatrical commission to make up a song for a specific activity. We had come to the end of our journey and were now looking to find a song that could encompass all of our feelings together and be used for a, potentially, moving ritual.

The commission for the song really did need to have resonance above and beyond the moment that it was being created for. It was not just for the people creating it in the room they were creating it in, but needed to be sung while processing to the sea with the flowery farewell. Also we only had a short time to create it - perhaps 30 minutes. I had my accordion and Kate had a fiddle and there were six of us (all adults) in the room creating the song.

My initial response was to ask everyone to come up with one line of text, so that we would have a six line song. I was leading, or perhaps 'chairing', the song-writing session but was aware that as an adult group it would be a very different process from that when working with children or with a mixed adult/child group. The differences would be in the speed of creativity and the deliberation and tone of the discussion. Children come up with ideas very easily they often don't worry too much about what others will think of their ideas. This observation is a generalisation but important to note. However adults, again generally, are much more self-conscious and more deliberate. They come with more social and personal baggage than children!

So although my first request to the group was 'to write one line about how we felt about the journey and getting to the sea', for some this was quite a difficult question, especially when they were being asked to find a line in only a few minutes. I therefore had to negotiate this session carefully, making sure that the quick thinkers and writers didn't make the more deliberate ones feel pressured into creating something that they did not feel was quite right. However, we did come up with a set of lines and then managed - together - to create a single stanza as follows. It had some rhymes, stories and possibilities. It had half-rhymes too - sea/sky and live/breath and a real sense of a shared work.

Open Space

Open space

Connecting lives and stories

Wide expanse

Of many possibilities

Sea going out

Out to sea

Sun going down

Merging with the sky

No longer waiting to live

Feeling alive with each breath

I then suggested that we find a tune in a similar way to how we found a tune for other songs on the project (including 'The Beginning' and 'Come Dye With Me'). This was by using a chance system through playing hand chimes ('The Beginning') or a random translation system through using the letters in the words to make a set of pitches for the melody ('Come Dye With Me'). Some of the group thought this was a good suggestion, as they had also heard those other songs and realised that in this way you could come up with something a bit unexpected, and out of the ordinary.

However, one of the group felt very strongly that the melody, and the ideas for the melody, should come from us, from the group and from an individual singing of each of the lines. This person was very clear that she felt we should not use a chance system and the rest of the group, who did not have strong opinions as to how we should create this song, agreed to go along with this.

We then proceeded to create the song line by line with each person in turn creating a new bit of melody. I made sure that if people did not feel comfortable in singing then they could suggest that we repeat a melodic line and similarly the group was very clear in keeping me on track - for instance 'connecting lives and stories' has a similar melody to 'of many possibilities' but with the last three notes different. I kept singing it wrong and the group kept putting me right!

The end-result seemed to work well. We found a melody that didn't quite end. It seemed to end on a cliff-edge (or the dominant chord for the musically literate) meaning that you wanted to hear it start again. It was a cyclical song, with a fiddle intro and accordion accompaniment. It was definitely a more adult song than a children's song and a world away from 'Another World' at the start of the project some nine months earlier. We were able to reflect that a group of adults creating a song by themselves will have a very different outcome from a song written by a group of adults and children working together, even if the end-result is to be sung by both adults and children together.

It felt as though the song worked for what it was designed for. In grey skies and the gloaming we went to the sea singing the words while carrying the flowers and said goodbye to the project.

How long will these songs last?

Who is the keeper of the songs?

What do these songs now mean to those who created them?

Hugh

119

Part Three
The Evaluation

Measuring things we can't measure

A pleasure it is, to find a Treasure

Measuring things we cannot measure. Having deeply, a being to turn to,

when our spirits says we have to.

Sometimes the pace in our trip need a lift.

A bone; fit to the back to make swift

A friend is a name to treasure, In conviction, we but cannot measure

Friendship; a prized gift Not Greek, but to give life a lift

Packing our lives with thrills,

And splendour, poise and bliss.

Mother earth becomes lively

A healthier and jovial abode Indeed pleasure it is to find a friend.

Raymond Anyanwu [1]

Why evaluate?

Measurement is the first step that leads to control and eventually to improvement. If you can't measure something, you can't understand it. If you can't understand it, you can't control it. If you can't control it, you can't improve it.

H. James Harrington [2]

Without evaluation it is hard to accumulate evidence which contributes to understanding the benefits of a project, particularly when that project is arts based and concerned with social issues.

With simple issues, few questions and fewer variables, evaluation can be a straightforward business. Measuring the effects of an arts project is more complex because there are so many interactions, creative improvisations, impromptu happenings and other variables. How many of the benefits of an arts project are directly because of the individual story making, art, music workshops and how much the mixture of arts activities? How do the individual people, social interactions, the environment, the weather and the food contribute? The 'river expedition's' success was a dynamic mix of all the elements which together shaped the project. When there are many different things to assess and many ways to measure any particular approach to evaluation can never reflect the whole project or its outcomes.

We are complex social creatures and have myriad of ways of being creative and interactive – or not. Yet with a well-planned, thoughtful project a diverse group of people can be brought together safely to share positive new creative experiences. To know that we are all unboxable and uncategorisable to some extent is no reason not to evaluate and to ask: what is valuable? Artists do evaluate though they may call it 'reflection'. A real time benefit of a more formal evaluation is that it brings focus and structure to the reflective practice which is essential for creativity itself.

The project asked a series of questions about the effect of doing creative activities, finding out more about where you live and if being with other mixed-heritage families and peers was a valuable, change experience with lasting benefits. A film maker documented each event and has made a series of short films about each one for Blazing Tales.

The project used quantitive and qualitive approaches to evaluation to gain insight into what worked and to provide a baseline from which to develop future work.

Quantitative *research asks very specific questions which participants are asked to answer by ticking a particular box or marking a number on a scale. This generates 'numerical data' which can be analysed as statistics. Small projects, like the 'river exe-pedition', do not have sufficient people involved to generate statistically significant results, but do provide worthwhile information about the projects effectiveness.*

Qualitative *research, looks for themes, and individual responses to broad questions and collects 'word data' and 'quotations' from participants. Such 'anecdotal' evidence is often dismissed as 'weak' research. Here where the subject of investigation includes hidden histories and the power of narrative it is poetic that 'anecdote' literally means 'unpublished' or 'never given out'. Our 'anecdotes' are the witness statements of people who were there. In the legal system such testimonies are considered very strong evidence.*

Alternating both approaches sets the 'soft' outcomes of the individual voices of participants alongside the 'harder' outcomes about satisfaction, learning and change.

Devising a questionnaire for a project allows for specific, relevant questions to be asked. Using a more widely recognised evaluation method may make a stronger case about a project's value. Where improving wellbeing and exploring social and emotional issues are part of a projects aims a broadly mental health based measuring method is desirable. Unfortunately there are few simple to use and score questionnaires for adults and children. Those most frequently used in health settings focus rather more on difficulties and mental ill health than positive mental health. The best fit with the 'river exe-pedition' project was the Warwick-Edinburgh Mental Well-being Scale (WEMWBS). This is a scale of positively worded items, used for assessing a population's mental wellbeing. See page 190 for more about this.

Evaluation is a structured way of investigating what happens during a project, and why. It involves gathering information as evidence before, during and after a project. The evidence can then be used to make judgements about what happened, why, and what effects it had. The evidence can also help improve how a project runs, help decide what works well and what might be done differently next time.

Arts Council England [3] provides helpful information on evaluating arts projects aspects of which are included in the summary below.

The four key phases in the monitoring and evaluation cycle are:
1. Planning. 2. Monitoring. 3. Evaluating. 4. Using the findings.

Evaluating helps:
- plan and clarify aims.
- to make changes and avoid disasters as a project unfolds.
- ensure quality is maintained.
- evidence the value of a project.
- document a projects contribution to the field/ sector.
- disseminate findings.
- collect evidence to support future funding applications.

Most evaluation is based on three key intentions:
1. Making judgements, based on evidence, about the value and quality of a project.
2. Being open and clear and involving all partners, including the people taking part.
3. Helping decision-making during a project and for future projects.

Evaluation has two main purposes:
1. Improving practice during a project and inform future projects.
2. Showing what happened as a result of a project.

Informing and improving is important so:
- projects can evolve and change.
- artists, group leaders and participants can see the evaluation is for their benefit, and not just for funders.

- projects can be as good or better next time and standards can be maintained or raised.

- all involved can develop new skills, interests, knowledge or insights.

The intention is to show how:

- arts projects can be a good way of learning.

- the people involved benefited from the project.

- what didn't work so well can be amended and learnt from.

- the funding has been well used.

Karen Huckvale.

Evaluation Outcomes
Exford

This weekend was arranged and led by the Planet Rainbow Project and Blazing Tales were contracted to lead the arts activities. Therefore the evaluation for this project stands alone. Here are some typical comments from the 14 families who attended.

What was the best part of the weekend at Exford?

The residential was described by a 12 year old as being *a very cool and groovy weekend.* Parents also repeated that the environment gave us and our children the opportunity to have individual space. The whole weekend had a real community feeling with everyone working together and producing art in various forms. Underlying the art activities it was evident that meeting people in similar circumstances i.e. with mixed-heritage families who my child and I could feel totally naturally with was an important part of the experience.

The activities were enjoyed by children, young people and their parents which naturally went along with building relationships and a sense of community.

What did you like doing?

One mother wrote, *Sara's morning exercises, seeing my daughter making friends, living with other people. I love the outdoor activities – just to play. It's pure joy to see Hugh's songs developing.* There was a general feeling of enjoying the music, being with other families, very relaxing. Several children mentioned the writing activities and being outside and getting to know more people. Another liked doing the boats and the food.

Repeated comments were made about the benefits of being outside, and the pleasure of parents seeing their children play and make new friends.

Any other comments?

We really had such a good time. I feel totally lifted...My son had a complete break from T.V. etc. Blazing Tales were wonderful in boosting his confidence. It was great for me to see my shy son participate in activities.

This weekend has been wonderful from start to finish - Sara, Hugh and Cara 'held the space' for us so beautifully - there was never an awkward empty moment, but it also felt fine to opt out. Blazing Tales were great!

Our son made a new friend, as did our daughter. The environment gave us, and them, the opportunity to have individual space.

What didn't you like?

All the answers echoed that leaving was hard. Thinking about leaving, leaving on Sunday and that two days wasn't long enough.

What could have made it better?

The overwhelming majority of people said things like knowing that we could do another weekend soon, or maybe do it twice/ thrice a year.

One person made an interesting suggestion - *I would have been good to spend time studying things like the wild birds in the garden.* A weekend goes pretty quickly and one person would have liked it if it had been one day longer.

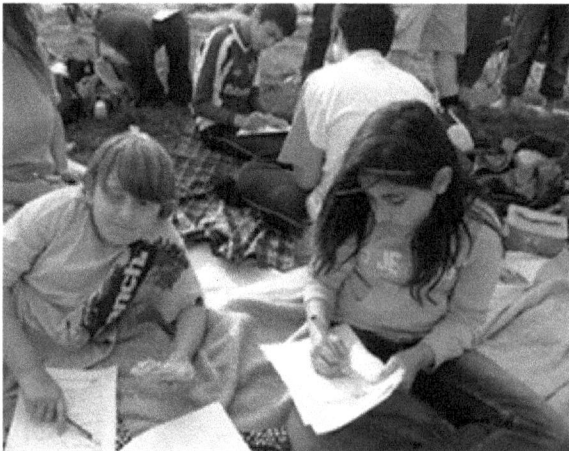

Filling out questionnaires

Exe Valley Weekend

Adult and young people's responses.

It's so nice not to feel conspicuous – to be taken for who we are – not what we look like. In a village where my son is the only ethnic minority child in his school it's really hard to ever feel like you are seen through the same filters as everyone else.

Responses to the workshops

VISUAL ART

Did you find the workshop:

Interesting & enjoyable	Good	Ok	Alright	Boring
12	0	0	0	0

Was the leader easy to understand?

Yes	Mostly	No
12	0	0

Did you learn anything new?

Yes, a lot	Yes, a bit	Not really	No
12	0	0	0

If Yes, what was it?
Nearly everybody clearly stated how they really enjoyed the whole process of natural plant dyeing from beginning to end, how easy it was to use the plants around us, what plants gave which colours, learning about the materials needed and science of it, and the different effects that can be achieved.
With the indigo dye they enjoyed the fixing, wax, creating patterns, unpicking the cloth and seeing the result.
This went along with learning how we can use nature around us to be creative.

What did you like the best?
This was a very popular activity, the group liked doing something new.
Also that there was no pressure. It was mentioned how well Cara had organised it, that she was very sharing and there was space to ask and explore.
The majority mentioned the process and experience of: unwrapping the fabrics, seeing the colours appear, and singing the indigo song while the dipping was happening.

What did you like the least?
Four (out of six) people made more positive comments about it all being great and wanting to do more. One person said it was very messy and they got very blue hands and one person mentioned sewing.

Do you want to add anything else?

- *Loved it so much. I want to be much more creative now. It was great that my children played whilst I was able to create.*
- *Having a practical art activity running throughout the weekend gives a lovely project to do when you have a spare moment.*
- *No, it was wonderful – thank you, I wish I had more time to do more.*

STORY WORK

Did you find the workshop....

Interesting & enjoyable	Good	Ok	Alright	Boring
8	2	0	0	0

Was the leader easy to understand?

Yes	Mostly	No
10	0	0

Did you learn anything new?

Yes, a lot	Yes, a bit	Not really	No
6	4	0	0

If Yes, what was the new thing learnt?
The group were very positive about learning more about local history, listening to the indigo story and learning about the life of Mary Baker (Princess Caribou from Witheridge), they liked the local stories.

Two people said they learnt about structuring and writing a story and how the guidance helped them overcome apprehension, and also how they learnt a number of ways to develop and finish an idea. Another person said they had learnt a lot from talking and listening to others.

What did you like the best?
Around half of the comments said they liked the storyteller, that her skill at it was great and that it had a good pace and gentle nature. One person said they liked being in the moment and bringing the imagination to life, others also enjoyed being inventive, the creative process and learning the tools to complete a project.
One person commented on watching the demonstrations and the devising process and another liked the local history aspect. Everything was also an answer.

What did you like the least?
Four people said there was nothing they didn't like, the other comments were practical due to weather and conditions: muddy track, smoke and rain.

What could be better?
Several people mentioned having longer time to develop their stories, others said nothing and the weather again.
There were some suggestions, which were:

> *Maybe put people into groups rather than let them do this themselves – would promote more mixing? Not really sure.*

> *Would use more visuals or objects to illustrate the stories.*
> *A longer walk.*

MUSIC

Did you find the workshop

Interesting & enjoyable	Good	Ok	Alright	Boring
12	1	0	0	0

Was the leader easy to understand?

Yes	Mostly	No
13	0	0

Did you learn anything new?

Yes a lot	Yes a bit	Not really	No
9	4	0	0

If Yes what was it?

Just always marvel how Hugh makes great songs from a few phrases and notes.

Lots of other comments spoke about learning different techniques to achieve making music, that the end result is still a work in progress, how to write lyrics and different techniques for writing melodies. People felt more confident to go about writing a song and felt that the music wasn't difficult and was open to everybody. Another person noted learning to work collaboratively and having permission to write, and be silly in songs. It was mentioned how the smallest thing can be an inspiration for creativity.

The indigo song was noted in particular:
How evocative the indigo song was probably because we had been so involved with it.

What did you like the best?
I loved everything about it. The whole event was a big sing song. What a wonderful way to spend a weekend!

There were three main points made:
- The first being how everyone was involved and the process was very inclusive as well as it being easy to join in.
- Secondly how people enjoyed Hugh's workshops and teaching style. His fluidity, expertise and ease- his cheery, approachable and lively musical character and how he was brilliant with the kids. One person said they found the confidence to take part in the singing, and another how there was no right or wrong way.
- Thirdly it was noted how some enjoyed singing and playing the finished songs, and the sound of the chime bars.

What did you like the least?

Four people said nothing or they didn't want to miss anything. One person said they didn't like the leader's skunk impressions!

Do you want to add anything else?

Loved it, it was fab, thank-you.

The music didn't stop (fantastic). Love the songs around the camp fire. It was lovely to fall asleep while people were singing, and one afternoon I woke up to the sound of a caterpillar. I loved it!

PRACTICAL INFORMATION

Everybody thought that the venue had been well chosen and was a stimulating and wonderful place to be. Most participants said the food was great with a couple describing it as really nice. Overwhelmingly, it was felt that information about the event had been given in a useful way.

Was where we held this event

A wonderful place to be	Well chosen	Stimulating	Boring	Poorly chosen	Not right
12	6	7	0	0	0

Was the food:

Great	Really nice	Good enough	Could be better	Poor	Awful
12	2	0	0	0	0

Was the information about the event given in a useful way?

Yes	Mostly	No
12	1	0

What did you like the best?

Many of the adults mentioned enjoying the friendly atmosphere, knowing their children were having a wonderful time and forming friendships, being creative and meeting new people. They made new friendships too, liked this, and it was clear people were enjoying each other's company.

Parents felt supported by being in a group and enjoyed the freedom of the place and lack of pressure. This included being cooked for and being in a beautiful venue, some liked it that the farm encouraged sustainability. The gentle and non-intrusive atmosphere was frequently mentioned.

Positive comments were made about enjoying making things: stories, music and craft, guessing riddles and making music and the songs, as well as the energy of the artists.

What did you like the least?
Most people commented on the weather, One person was sorry to miss the late night campfires as they had to go to sleep with their child.
Another felt that having some children who were already very close took away from others being able to shine or bond, sometimes.

What could have been better?
Practical things like the washing facilities were mentioned by one person, however it was alright for the weekend. Several people said they would like it to be longer, that it was perfect and that they wouldn't change anything.

Would you like to say anything else?
These comments were extremely positive and many people said they'd like to come back again and that we should consider doing it annually. Some quotes below show how people felt.

I loved it and feel it has enhanced my life in a most transformative way.

I have really enjoyed spending time with my family and mixing with other families.

I liked the way everyone joined in most of the activities and it felt like a community. At the same time it felt ok to drop out of something if you didn't feel in the mood- like the story walk (in my case) Having the photographer was ok because he was unobtrusive and friendly.

This weekend and other times like this are invaluable for me as the white parent of a mixed heritage child for support and interaction and relaxation and for my daughter to be in an open and accepting environment.

I've had a wonderful weekend, thank you for all your lovely efforts, thoughtfulness and ease with which you held the camp.

I have been made to feel very welcome despite not being part of Planet Rainbow or living in Devon. Really appreciate the support from other adults with my child who finds it difficult in groups sometimes.

I am very grateful for this experience. Please can we come back again!

KNOWING MORE ABOUT WHERE YOU LIVE

How has exploring Devon and the River Exe affected you?

More connected to Devon	Nothing new	Know more about history/ nature/ culture	Will explore more in future	Prefer the towns/cities	Other
6	0	9	9	0	0

How was it being with other mixed-heritage families?

Interesting	A relief	A pleasure	It makes no difference to me	Comfortable	Too intense	Other
6	3	7	4	7	0	0

Was it a change from your usual experience of living in Devon?

Yes	Mostly	No
10	2	2

Have you made any new friends?

Yes	I think so	No
10	4	0

Would you come on an event like this again?

Yes	Probably	Possibly	No
13	1	0	0

Could you say something about being with other mixed-heritage families?

So glad not to feel alone and meeting like-minded people is wonderful.

Could talk about things unselfconsciously- good and bad things about living in dual/mixed heritage families. E.g could tell someone my son was upset on world book day because he couldn't think who to dress up as for school- that "Harry Potters not brown" without being told "my son wants to go as Yoda - but he's not green".

Really important to be one of many rather than unique. Nearly all groups/friends that we know are 'all white'.

All my family grew up in West Yorkshire so were always in mixed heritage groups at school and found it quite a change arriving in Devon which is very white.

Living in the city we do see other mixed heritage families however to spend time in this environment together is a real encouragement.

Slightly. My children have been exposed to more mixed heritage children than ever before.

This was a very special event in the way the space was held by the organisers. It felt supportive and nourishing.

It was good to see the children building relationships with others like themselves.

I know and interact with other mixed heritage families.

Usually me and my son would often go to things and we would be the only mixed heritage family - so really lovely to be in a context where we were the norm and not "unusual".

Could you say anything else about the whole experience?

The adults enjoyed making things and learning new skills and one found the experience 'magical'.

The support from being with other mixed-heritage families was re-iterated, and there is something captured in their own words:

I feel it has been a real confidence builder for my children to spend time with other children from similar backgrounds.

It's so nice not to feel conspicuous – to be taken for who we are – not what we look like. In a village where my son is the only ethnic minority child in his school it's really hard to ever feel like you are seen through the same filters as everyone else. Just being with mixed heritage families helps to normalise our experience.

One person felt there was something missing, an opportunity missed.
I felt there was a lack of acknowledgement around the more "invisible" heritage of our children, so an opportunity missed to celebrate and bring alive the diversity of our children's backgrounds. I feel our kids are already surrounded by English culture on a daily basis and it is their other mix that often is unspoken, therefore not alive for them in the everyday.

Another person said finding out more about the history of black and minority ethnic people living in Devon was very educational.

Key point: Being with other mixed-heritage families

The team noted that for some people it was extremely important to be with other mixed-heritage families, whereas for others it was just a nice experience anyway. This broad spread of attitudes and reasons for being there involved complex negotiation for the team throughout the weekend. Whilst some parents were desperate to talk, others weren't and we felt most sensitive to children being around who did not want to be there just because they were mixed-heritage.

This was an early event, with more to come, and a lot of newness for everyone. It was decided not to hold a talking session about mixed-ness on this camp and to go for a relaxed approach that invited a culture of free expression. There were countless informal and fascinating conversations between people who wanted to talk. Parents freely shared their experiences of being in a mixed-heritage family and parenting with mixed-heritage children who were growing up in Devon. The children were observed chatting more than they would usually do about their similarities and differences during play. The children shared in their own way and at their own pace and level of interest just like the adults. Parminder was active in encouraging parents to share their experiences and find mutual support. The dyeing and sewing actively supported an intimate, relaxed chatting-whilst-making atmosphere.

For this event the team decided to encourage an informal approach to discussion about living in a mixed-heritage family.

To enable:

> Sharing experientially.
> Settling in to a new group and managing expectation.
> Best use of time.
> Parents discussing their children within earshot.
> Young people talking and opening up with parents around.
> Children who generally prefer to be active.
> Negotiating a broad range of needs and expectations.
> Managing varying levels of interest in the subject.

Following on from this event, and responding to specific feedback the team discussed how and where we could incorporate a discussion time to create a conducive, private space for discussion in an outside camp situation. At the next event an adult conversation was arranged whilst other activities were taking place for the children. The plan was to hold a similar discussion for young people at the following event. Unfortunately due to constraints of time, space and activities the group unanimously decided not to do so when given the option. Interestingly, by the last event the urgency to discuss these issues had dissipated and relationships had developed within all age groups.

Exe Valley Weekend
Under 13's responses

I learnt more about dyeing through the song.

I learnt that you can eat a flower.

I would really like to do this more often.

GENERAL INFORMATION

Age and gender.
A total of 14 children and young people attended the whole camping weekend, between the ages of 1-13+ years old. 2 were under 5 years old and the rest between 7 and 13 +. 2 visiting children came for the day on Saturday and did not fill in a form.

Eleven under 13's were girls, and 3 under 13's were boys.

How old are you?

1-2 years	3-4 years	5-6 years	7-8 years	9-10years	11-12 years	13 + years
1	1	0	2	4	4	2

Responses to the workshops

VISUAL ART

Did you find the workshop...

Interesting & enjoyable	Good	Ok	Alright	Boring
8	1	1	0	1

Was the leader easy to understand?

Yes	Mostly	No
8	1	1

Did you learn anything new?

Yes, a lot	Yes, a bit	Not really	No
4	5	0	1

If Yes, what did you learn?
Everything about dyeing; you can use plants for dyeing; identifying different plants; looking for which plants you can use for dyeing; how to dye cloth with natural dye.

I learnt about Indigo and making; about waxing and dyeing fabric; about the Indigo dyes and drilling holes in wood to make buttons.

What did you like the best? Most children said they liked making their bags and dyeing with the indigo, including when their hands turned blue, waxing and scratching the wax off the cloth. They liked the indigo song too. One person said nothing and another said everything.

What did you like the least? Four people said nothing, another mentioned waiting whilst there were some comments about threading needles and sewing taking too long.

What could be better? Most people said nothing, or more of the same – meaning they would like to do more. One child said their sewing could be better.

Do you want to add anything else?
Didn't really do any. Helped mum a bit. Would have liked to have done the dyeing but was busy playing and filming.

Cara just provides such a range of resources with patience and gentleness coupled with such skill & knowledge.

(The last response was written by the parent of a three year old who, having talked with her child, added these comments.)
We were happy that some children enjoyed playing in a free and fantastic environment while making new friends. This was part of the resources on offer.

STORYWORK

Did you find the workshop...

Interesting & enjoyable	Good	Ok	Alright	Boring
6	1	3	0	1

Was the leader easy to understand?

Yes	Mostly	No
9	1	0

Did you learn anything new?

Yes, a lot	Yes, a bit	Not really	No
2	6	2	1

If Yes, what was it? One person said they learnt how to make stories better, another that they learnt the stories themselves and one said about listening skills. Knowing more about history was mentioned and someone said I learnt that you can be inspired by taking walks out in the country side. The heightening of perception on the walk lead one child to want to share an observation from nature I saw a worm on a spider web.

What did you like the best? Most children said they liked listening to the stories, especially around the camp fire, and a younger one enjoyed watching everyone's reactions to the stories. Two children liked being able to write their own versions of the story, and two others liked the walk and making up stories on the walk. Working together with friends was also a point that was made.

What did you like the least? Three children said nothing and the other comments mentioned the mud on the walk. One child wrote about some annoying people.

What could be better? Two children said they'd like a longer walk and one said the walk could have been better, another mentioned the mud again. One didn't know and another said nothing.

Do you want to add anything else?
I really enjoyed this – my favourite activity.

I would really like to do this more often.

MUSIC
Did you find the workshop...

Interesting & enjoyable	Good	Ok	Alright	Boring
7	3	2	0	0

Was the leader easy to understand?

Yes	Mostly	No
11	1	

Did you learn anything new?

Yes, a lot	Yes, a bit	Not really	No
3	3	3	1

If Yes, what was it? Most people talked about learning to write songs in a group, creating words, making songs out of words. Most people enjoyed playing the instruments and trying different ones. One person learnt how to play a new instrument, another learnt more about dyeing through the song.

What did you like the best?

Singing and playing musical instruments.
Everything.
Playing songs round the camp fire.
Playing it in a fun way.
We got to sing.
Singing, doing music, hand chimes.
The songs.
Writing the Indigo song.
Being able to contribute to songs.
Joining in. It was fun.

What did you like the least? Three children said nothing, another didn't know. One couldn't see, another felt forced to play, one said the people with no rhythm. One person was embarrassed at their dad singing a solo, however it seemed liked by all.

What could be better? A lot of this group said nothing or that they wanted to do more. One person felt they needed to remember the songs better and one would like people to have better rhythm. One person felt there could be a better variety of instruments provided.

Do you want to add anything else?

Not really just that it was really good.
I really always enjoy music workshops.
Having music as a main activity but also as a background / constant theme gives such a feeling of fun, continuity & inclusiveness.

GENERAL COMMENTS

Did you learn anything new? One girl said she learnt that you can eat a flower, others were more practical and involved: making a fire and putting up a bell tent.

What did you like best? Tony gave out some Blackberry Phones for a few hours on Saturday for the children to take photos and short videos to record what they were doing. This was enormously popular and they liked using the phones to make videos and using the site trampoline.

What did you like the least? One person wrote, 'the meetings, I found them really boring.' Camp life was included in comments such as, 'didn't like going to bed or having to get up early.'

Do you want to add anything else? One child would like to make more fires, another that it was really good.

Key point: Playing
The farm was a wonderful place to be, and the owner enjoys people exploring and making the most of his land. We encouraged participation in the workshops and there was good take up, but we also allowed for children to just play if they wanted to. This flexibility was valued as a very positive part of the experience. As a family camp the responsibility ultimately lay with parents in this situation and we weren't making any child do anything they didn't want to.

Playing with other children like themselves felt like an excellent way to increase positive identity and encourage relaxed conversations about hair, travel, mum's, dad's, families and the other things about being mixed-heritage. The play was 'held' within the structure of the weekend and we asked everyone to gather for the group time, which wasn't always popular with the under 13's.

The River Bank Day

Adult and young people's responses.

I really like being around people like me. I don't know why anyone wouldn't want to be mixed. All my friends are white British but they don't make me feel different. They love my skin colour. Sorry I just wanted to let you know because a lot of people feel bad about being mixed in high school xxx☺

PRACTICAL

Was where we held this event:

A wonderful place to be	Well chosen	Stimulating	Boring	Poorly chosen	Not right
8	2	4	0	0	0

Was the food

Great	Really nice	Good enough	Could be better	Poor	Awful
5	4	1	1	0	0

Blazing Tales provided the basis for a picnic, people were asked to bring food to share.

Was the information about the event given in a useful way?

Yes	Mostly	No
7	4	0

What did you like the best?

There was a general feeling amongst the entire group of enjoying being outside in the surroundings and being near the river. Included in this was climbing trees and the sunshine, it all made for a very relaxing time; drawing, sketching by the river and being in good company. As one person said - the variety – art, music, stories & being outside! Another noted: It's hard to say but the instruments were fab & iridescent insects appeared that were fab. While making the crocodile was mentioned too.

What did you like the least?
Two main things were said by several people: the evaluation and form filling and the cows. One person found some moments boring.

What could have been better?
It was suggested there be more activities for older children, and that the place could have been better. One person said it was all good and another found nothing really could have been better.

Would you like to say anything else?
General comments were made about having a great day, with nice weather that they found very enjoyable. One person enjoyed talking to people.

One of the 13-16 year olds wanted to say more about mixed-ness, because we had initiated a parent discussion group. In their own words;

When we were talking about being a mixed family involve a few of the older children. Plus I really liked being around people like me. I don't know why anyone wouldn't want to be mixed. All my friends are white British but they don't make me feel different. They love my skin colour. Sorry I just wanted to let you know because a lot of people feel bad about being mixed in high school xxx☺

SOCIAL

How was it being with other mixed – heritage families?

Interesting	A relief	A pleasure	It makes no difference to me	Comfortable	Too intense	Other
3	1	3	4	4	0	1

Was it a change from your usual experience of living in Devon?

Yes	Mostly	No
2	3	4

Could you say something about that?
One adult summed up the statement about it 'making no difference to me': Mostly it makes no difference as we find other 'others' but it was

great to be in a 'built for purpose' group. Others appreciated the environment in which they live in Devon.

We live in a place that's as nice as this. Natural surroundings. No shop!! Great.
Good to relax with people as opposed to working and 'working' on things together.

How has exploring Devon and the River Exe affected you?

More connected to Devon	Nothing new	Know more about history/ nature/ culture	Will explore more in future	Prefer the towns/ cities	Other
2	1	2	8	2	1

Could you say anything else about the experience?
Lovely surroundings.
Really relaxing.
Beautiful gift of a day.
It has been fun. And I have had a good time.
I learnt a lot about nature.

Responses to the workshops

STORYWORK

Did you find the workshop...

Interesting & enjoyable	Good	Ok	Alright	Boring
3	1	0	0	0

Was the leader easy to understand?

Yes	Mostly	No
4	0	0

Did you learn anything new?

Yes, a lot	Yes, a bit	Not really	No
1	1	2	0

If Yes, what was it?

How nice it is here.

More, but need more time to reflect on the day before I can formalise it in to words.

Another parallel story of Cinderella I'd never heard of.

What did you like the best?

The picnic, eating some shared multi – cultural food.

Hearing the stories making me want to go travelling.

Making the characters and being by the river.

What could be better?

Just to make sure we got the message it was mentioned again that the evaluation form was too long and someone wondered if there were other ways of doing it like expressing themselves.

Do you want to add anything else?

The great weather really supported the day.

VISUAL ART

Did you find the workshop...

Interesting & enjoyable	Good	Ok	Alright	Boring
2	1	0	0	0

Was the leader easy to understand?

Yes	Mostly	No
3	0	0

Did you learn anything new?

Yes, a lot	Yes, a bit	Not really	No
1	2	0	0

If Yes, what was it?

That my left hand was quite expressive. Would I trust that again? Maybe.

How to make stuff out of things around you.

Drawing with my left hand, quite an experience.

What did you like the best? The group liked paddling in the river and putting the crocodile together and everything about making the crocodile.

What did you like the least?
> *During the morning walk along the river Cara got the group drawing on stones, letting go of what had been made was difficult and someone said, throwing away my picture stone.*

Do you want to add anything else?
> *I could have quite easily stayed longer given the opportunity. Great!!*

MUSIC

Did you find the workshop...

Interesting & enjoyable	Good	Ok	Alright	Boring
1	1	1	0	0

Was the leader easy to understand?

Yes	Mostly	No
3	0	0

Did you learn anything new?

Yes, a lot	Yes, a bit	Not really	No
0	1	2	0

If Yes, what was it?
The gongs were a big feature of the music at this workshop and one person liked the vibration of the gongs.

What did you like the best?
It was liked that Hugh involves everyone when writing the songs, and encourages working together. One person also noted they liked the choice of instruments.

What did you like the least?
One person said they felt rushed.

What could be better?
Again one person felt that they would have preferred more time.

Key Point: The Evaluation Form

There was consistent negative feedback about the evaluation form. The group were very willing to participate in evaluating the project and understood why it was important to evaluate the arts and find out more about mixed-heritage families in Devon. There were some very lively conversations and tangible enthusiasm for the day and the project as a whole. However, the adult's verbal comments to us were not being matched by their written comments. We received overwhelmingly positive verbal feedback but this was not captured in the evidence we collected.

We thought that the feedback about the form should be responded to as we found it difficult to initiate and understood that there were lots of questions. It had resulted in the form being cursorily filled in, not completed or not returned. The team reflected that for a weekend it had seemed manageable, but for a day much less so. Sara decided a smaller form would lead to greater participation, maintain consistency but reduce the volume. Using film also formed part of the evaluation and we heard more lively feedback that way. This was a learning curve for us as well and we aimed to be flexible and responsive to feedback.

Key Point: Documentary Film

Film maker, Tony Walker documented this project through film and photography. Tony is also a workshop leader who facilitates participation on arts projects with film making and digital recording. However for this project his role was solely documentary. Tony was an intrinsic part of the team and his focus and positioning were part of our artistic planning and the artists and participants were all used to him being around; with the subtle skill of the film-maker.

Key Point: The Bullocks

Bullocks were a problem for part of the afternoon. The site had been visited twice by the team and the fact that the cattle visited the river at intervals had not been noticed during the reconnaissance because they weren't in the field at the time. It was a health and safety concern which the team responded to.

River Bank day
Under 13's responses

I liked the story about the girl, making charisma the crocodile and her song.

STORY WORK
Did you find the workshop...

Interesting and enjoyable	Good	Ok	Alright	Boring
3	1	0	0	1

Was the leader easy to understand?

Yes	Mostly	No
4	1	0

Did you learn anything new?

Yes, a lot	Yes, a bit	Not really	No
0	3	1	1

If Yes, what was it?

Blazing Tales work integrates art forms and the under 13's did not successfully discriminate in their answers to the different inputs, therefore in the story section there are comments like I learnt how to make sculpture out of things that you find on a beach and other places. Sara did add in crocodile facts during the day and one person noted, *I learnt more about crocodiles.*

What did you like the best?

The story about the girl with the horrible step mother was noted by two young people as being what they liked. Two others said about the sculpture and Making charisma the crocodile and her song. One person said Right now, the last minutes.

What did you like the least?

All except for one commented on not liking the cows or their poo. One didn't like the yappy dogs on the way & thought the cow was a monster behind the bush. Another complained about the walk.

What could be better?
The walk could be shorter, was suggested by one. One young child said:
We didn't get any toys.

Do you want to add anything else?
No more farms.
Possibly a reference to the animal contact in the day.

VISUAL ART
Did you find the workshop...

Interesting and enjoyable	Good	Ok	Alright	Boring
3	1	0	0	0

Was the leader easy to understand?

Yes	Mostly	No
3	0	0

Did you learn anything new?

Yes, a lot	Yes, a bit	Not really	No
1	1	2	0

If Yes, what was it?
One comment about sketching with left hand.

What did you like the best?
Creating the crocodile was a popular activity and it's mentioned throughout. So is drawing, sketching and climbing the tree.

What did you like the least?
Walking was noted.

MUSIC
Did you find the workshop...

Interesting and enjoyable	Good	Ok	Alright	Boring
1	2	0	0	0

Was the leader easy to understand?

Yes	Mostly	No
3	0	0

Did you learn anything new?

Yes, a lot	Yes, a bit	Not really	No
1	1	0	1

If Yes, what was it?
One person said they had learnt the Indonesian song. As another song was written another young person said they learnt how to put a song together.

What did you like the best?
One said they liked two songs, one was a young child's rhyme called The monkey, they also liked the song that was written, the croc song ☺
Another said they liked Listening ☺

River Bank reflective evaluation

Open discussion session on parenting led by Parminder Southcott

Five women attended and questions were asked to prompt discussion, sharing experiences and feelings on parenting mixed-heritage children. The discussion explored the difficulty of what to do or how to react when issues around identity and acceptance - presenting internally and externally – occur.

Negative points raised were:

- Low and negative self-value in children and young people.
- Low self-esteem in children and young people.
- Lack of contact with non-resident or general absence of black/ minority ethnic parent and their extended family.
- Lack of multiracial social networks.
- Lack of confidence in parenting of mixed-heritage children and young people.
- Lack of visual representation of black/ minority ethnic and mixed-heritage people within local communities.
- Lack of black/ minority ethnic and mixed-heritage people in the work place/delivering services (especially in childcare establishments).

- Lack of parenting black/ minority ethnic and mixed-heritage information and resources.
- Lack of support (or access to) in dealing with specific incidents (racial bullying + identity).
- Low numbers of support groups in rural and urban area and limited access to such groups where extant.
- Some feelings that diversity is seen as an add on to mainstream services.
- Some parents felt that the media inflicted negative black/ minority ethnic images to their children- especially those whose heritage is affected by current affairs for example those linked to the Arab world and the "war on terror".
- Some parents felt that a lack of understanding of both cultures, or when one culture was missing from their lives, meant their children didn't have a whole sense of self.

Positive points raised were:

- Some parents were able to draw on family and elders for support.
- Some parents had positive interactions with their children and were able to share positive stories of family and traditions.
- OFSTED was perceived to have got better at regulating diversity and equality in educational and child care settings.
- Devon was felt to be moving forward in its understanding and response to a multi-racial society but was behind other larger cities, such as Bristol.
- Exeter was felt to reflect a more visible multi-cultural society.
- Some parents didn't agree that there were any issues for their children and felt that their children were ok about their identity.
- All parents felt that greater access to support and activities exploring diversity and especially mixed-ness was a positive and much needed resource.
- Parents had confidence in partaking in activities exploring identity and self-esteem.
- Parents were pleased to have access to groups like Planet Rainbow Project and Blazing Tales and hoped they will become sustainable in order to continue providing a service and activities.

Exeter Day
Adult and young people's responses

Good to discover new bits of Exeter & history that I didn't know about.

Were the locations today...

New and Stimulating	Well chosen	Boring	Poorly chosen	Not family friendly
5	6	1	0	0

Was the information about the event given in a useful way?

Yes	Mostly	No
9	0	0

Is there anything else you want to add?

Two people declared they'd had a great or wonderful day. Two adults said how very interesting they had found it.

Others had enjoyed the day but commented I think it's sometimes difficult to please such a wide range of children, I think it was more suitable for my 7 year old than my 2 year old. This was echoed in the statement that the walk and talk was really interesting but a bit too long for the kids.

Big thanks were also given.

How was it being with other mixed-heritage families?

Interesting	A relief	A pleasure	It makes no difference to me	Comfortable	Too intense	Other
1	1	1	2	6	0	1 invaluable

Was it a change from your usual experience of living in Devon?

Yes	Mostly	No
3	3	2

How has exploring Devon and the River Exe affected you?

More connected to Devon	Nothing new	Know more about history/ nature/culture	Will explore more in the future	Prefer the countryside	Other
2	1	6	5	1	0

Could you say something about that?
There was an overall feeling that it was absolutely wonderful to be one of many rather than to be unusual, and that apart from other outings with Planet Rainbow we are almost always with all white families. There was a general recognition that we don't normally get such exposure to mixed families and how it was nice to feel different.

Two people said they hadn't found it that different for the following reasons: *Not really, but I don't go around on tours!* On the recurring theme of discovering more about where you live it was said - *I live in Exeter so it hasn't been too different, but I've never heard certain parts of the history of Exeter.*

It is clear that this event made the group feel closer to where they live, increased their knowledge and understanding and encouraged them to think about exploring more in the future. Two people said they preferred a different landscape or had not found anything new.

Could you say anything else about the experience?
There was a lot of enthusiasm for knowing more about Exeter and learning about it, with many comments like: *Good to discover new bits of Exeter & history that I didn't know about and showed me parts of Exeter I didn't know about.*

One person also mentioned going to known city spaces for the first time, I had never been to the Spacex Gallery before although have intended to for years. Nice to be at The Priory with a familiar group.

The intention behind the day about discovering Exeter's global links was clearly received. My daughter is mixed heritage and born in Devon as I was. I feel it is so important that she feels she has a connectedness with Devon as well as the connections with Jamaica, Nigeria and London.

What did you like the best?
Five out of seven comments chose The Priory as the best part of the day. This was coupled with the walk by two people. Another two preferred the morning workshop with the art and poem writing.
>*I liked everything, enjoyed everything.*

What did you like the least?
>*Standing on a pavement beside a busy road with an unruly 5 year old.*
>*Walking around!*

What could've been better?
>The same young voices said, *Making the walking time not as long, and not doing it in Exeter because it's embarrassing and it makes me want to go shopping.*

Would you like to say anything else?
Most people said Thank You!
>*Really enjoyed the whole day – expressing self, history and the tea & cake!*
>*Great day out with my boy!*
>*Each event has left me with a sense of well-being and wanting more. I feel it is an important part of my daughter's sense of self and identity to regularly spend time with other people of mixed heritage and black/minority/ ethnic. We attend various other groups which are almost totally mono culture.*

Did you find the workshops...

Interesting & enjoyable	Good	Ok	Alright	Boring
4	2	1	0	0

Were the leaders easy to understand?

Yes	Mostly	No
6	1	0

One added the comment - *All were wonderful, inspiring, friendly and approachable.*

Did you learn anything new?

Yes, a lot	Yes, a bit	Not really	No
4	3	0	0

If Yes, what was did you learn that was new?
One person wrote about the creative aspect - To make and play music, to create some craft, to experience the oral tradition of storytelling.
Everyone else focused on the historical element of the day:

> *Learnt about life in the Tudor times.*
> *History of parts of Exeter.*
> *Trade routes.*
> *Tudor dance.*
> *That the clock figure is Henry VIII and the forgotten cemetery riots.*

What did you like best?

About it all?
> *Not a typical day out.*
> *Made a nice change.*
> *Children dressing up in Tudor clothes.*

Music?
> *Song about the aunt.*
> *Fun as usual.*
> *Good to break the ice.*

Art?
> *Doing the self-portraits.*
> *Inspirational.*
> *Being creative.*

Story Work?
> *Writing the stuff for the I D cards.*
> *The moral of the story.*

It was not a typical day out and from these comments it appears all aspects of the day were enjoyed, with there being something for everyone at different times through the day.

The Crab Walk was not favoured by younger children or parents of younger children, but they had a good experience dressing up and playing at The Priory, and doing the creative activities in the morning.

As the group rambled down onto the busy Exeter Quay on a warm Saturday afternoon I noticed heads turning at our cultural and colour mix as we walked past, and our relaxed, confident children walked through the crowds. I overheard comments of 'where have they all come from?' and 'I've never seen so many brown kids in one go.' Our straggly groups of families and clusters of children did stand out from the crowd but they were so caught up in each other and the crab walk that they didn't seem to notice, or care. The on-lookers had no idea that as a passing white woman bringing up the rear I might be with them or interested in what they said.

Exeter
Under 13's responses

Did you find the workshops...

Really great	Good	Ok	Alright	Boring
4	2	1	0	2

Were the leaders easy to understand?

Yes	Mostly	No
3	5	1

Did you learn anything new?

Yes, a lot	Yes, a bit	Not really	No
6	1	1	1

If yes, what new thing did you learn?
Stuff about the Tudors and all what Phil said.
About Tudors – what they wore, what they traded etc.
About poems.

What did you like best?
The comments were quite random and one even harked back to the camping weekend. They reflect a mixed bag of what had been liked best.

About it all?
The friendliness.
The drawing.
The camping.
The walk, I don't have favourites.

The workshops?
The identity card music writing.
Funny songs.
Drawing myself.
The painting pictures.

What did you like the least?

About it all?
The walking thing with Phil cause I was tired.
Eating the weevil biscuit.
Long talks.
Not enough doing stuff.

What could be better?
From these comments it appears that the under 13's were less at ease with this day and that the activities didn't suit them as much as previously. Having established a culture of being out in the countryside, making art and playing it was clear that they prefer to do that!

About it all?
More arty things.
More interesting.
Shorten the long talks.
More writing songs.

Exmouth
Adult and young people's responses

I liked the interweaving of arts – music, craft, story, with the locations and sense of individual and collective experiences.

Were the locations today...

New and stimulating	Well chosen	Boring	Poorly chosen	Not family friendly
3	5	0	0	0

Were the food arrangements...

Great	Really nice	Good enough	Could be better	Poor	Awful
0	3	4	0	0	0

Was the information about the event given in a useful way?

Yes	Mostly	No
6	0	0

Is there anything else you want to add?
There were unanimous comments of, *another fantastic day*

How was it being with other mixed heritage families?

Interesting	A relief	A pleasure	It makes no difference	Comfortable	Too intense	Other
1	0	4	2	1	0	0

How has exploring Devon and the River Exe affected you?

More connected to Devon	Nothing new	Know more About history/ nature/culture	Will explore more in future	Prefer the countryside	Other
4	1	6	3	0	0

Can you say something about being with other mixed-heritage families?

Forget that there are in fact a few present here.
Nice to really feel presence in 'quintessential' England.
Loved the boat ride and conversations.

Could you say anything else about the experience?

Forged a link with some of these places.
Lovely memories!
Enriching.

What did you like the best?

Most people really enjoyed the mixture of arts activities and the group feeling of meeting up and creating together again was evident at the last event.

Seeing everyone again.
All, singing, stories, boat trip, company.
Music and song writing.
The interweaving of arts – music, craft, story, with locations and sense of individual and collective experiences.
The boat trip.

Did you find the workshops...

Interesting and enjoyable	Good	Ok	Alright	Boring
6	2	0	0	0

Comment: *great & fun*

Were the leaders easy to understand?

Yes	Mostly	No
6	0	0

Did you learn anything new?

Yes, a lot	Yes, a bit	Not really	No
1	4	1	0

If yes, what did you learn?

Several adults liked the bits on the boat about local history, a couple of people equally mentioned working as a team and another person specifically talked about the collaborative writing process. Also mentioned were learning two new stories and being able to 'express myself.'

What did you like the best?
About it all?
Most people said they liked everything, others spoke of groups interacting. A sense of friendship and group cohesion came through. One person summed it up like this, a sense of fluidity of leading days – held & structured, & yet very relaxed.

Music?
1 adult thought it was very good, and another liked playing the violin and the drumming workshop most of all.

Art and Story
Were summed up as beautiful and very expressive.

Exmouth
Under 13's responses

Did you find the workshops...

Were the leaders easy to understand?

Yes	Mostly	No
4	4	0

Did you learn anything new?

If Yes, what did you learn that was new?
Making a garland.
The story.
The friendship with Y.
Loads of stuff.
That everything has beauty.

What did you like the best?

About it all?
On the boat.

Going down to the beach and putting the garland in the sea.
Throwing in the garland.

Music?

It was funny.
That it had a very Caribbean-ish Tune. It was great.

Art?

It was fun. Because I like making things.
Everything has beauty. Lovely.

Story?

It was weird.
Always has a sort of moral.   Nice.

What did you like the least?

About it all?

Getting splinters on my hands when getting the leaves.
The boat trip was too short.

What could be better?
About it all:

Everybody said nothing could be better, with the exception of one who suggested it could have more drama because: 'I love drama and I think that would be really fun.'

The 'river exe-pedition'
Project conclusions.

General

It's so nice not to feel conspicuous – to be taken for who we are – not what we look like. In a village where my child is the only ethnic minority child in the school it's really hard to ever feel like you are seen through the same filters as everyone else.

Here is a record of the whole evaluation written through the questions that were asked on the form. There is a mixture of quantitive tables for the whole project and qualitative results alongside observations that have been made based on the information. As an independent project this group of people was self-referring, they chose to attend for the benefit of themselves and their family. It is hoped that these findings can help identify ways to recognise need, provide further support and create opportunities for individuals and families which can be taken up by: arts, social, community, education, heritage, environmental and health agencies.

A total of 104 places were taken during the 'exe-pedition' over four events. Of those places 47 were adults and 57 were young people under the age of 13. Within the adults 12 were fathers and 35 were mothers, within the under 13's 18 were boys and 39 were girls. Adults: 47, men: 12, women: 35. Under 13's: 57, girls: 39, boys: 18. This made up around 15 families with a core group of 12 families. Out of those 12 families over half came to 3 or more events. Around 2/3rds of the families were single-mother households.

There were two sets of forms, one for adults and one for under 13's. The 13-15 year olds who attended filled out the 'adult' forms.

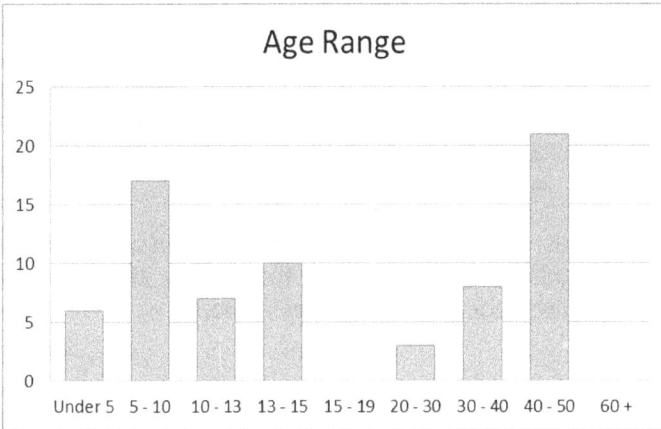

Age Range

The majority of children who took part were between the ages of 5-10, from the detail of each event it is shown that most were between 7-10 years old.

No young people between the ages of 15-19 attended.

Most adults were in their 40's with the fewest being parents in their 20's.

Working with families and a mixed age range is both a joy and a challenge.

Some positive impacts are:

> Less age categorized experience which is common within schools and clubs.

> Experiencing and shaping self-defining groups within, and across, age groups.

> Creating a culture of mutual support between families and individuals.

Some limitations are:

> Not providing consistency for the needs of specific age groups.

> Managing family dynamics and behaviour where parents are responsible for their own child.

In this workshop series we tried to provide a variety of activities for all ages. Some events were subtly pitched to be more suitable for different ages. Families booked to come in advance, a low fee was charged, and this indicated to us who was coming, however unexpected last minute changes could tip the balance. For example, the Exeter day was better suited for young people, and quite a few much younger ones came. The river bank day was ideal for younger children and quite a few 10-14's came. This is the unpredictable element of hosting a self-referring community event. The activities were still enjoyed and offered a memorable experience but example the vagaries of working with family groups and last minute changes.

Some hoped for areas for development were discussed by the participants and recognised together with the artists through the experience of running mixed-age group family workshops.

> To extend the service specifically for young people, aged 12-18. To provide a safe, arts based space for mixed-heritage young people to come together. To continue working creatively in outside environments and giving them the opportunity to be more self-directed and have greater input.

> To create 'making and talking' spaces. Making private spaces for specific age/peer groups to be together working on creative projects and handling their own mixed-heritage issues in the ways they want to. Including time for young children as well as adults or parents.

> To have a culturally diverse team of artists and facilitators to act as guides and role-models.

Firstly, creating a conducive environment to talk openly within a family situation was problematic. For eg: having a parental discussion with children in earshot; having group discussion time when not everyone present was interested to do so; to encourage young people to open up and talk with their parents, carers, siblings close by.

Secondly, the outside spaces we were using were places where we organised one off events. They were not part of centres or community spaces. Therefore we made best use of what was available to us within the limitations. Opportunities to become familiar with the places wasn't possible, which can increase a feeling of ownership and confidence in the users.

Thirdly, to continue this work it would be vital to employ a more culturally diverse team of artists and facilitators to act as role-models and guides. Particularly mixed-heritage adults or young people and where the potential exists for children to be in contact with people who share the same home culture, especially where a parent, or extended family are absent. Beyond that, for the group to enjoy the positive social diversity it represents.

By the end of the project the parent participants and some young people had all said they would value having a young people's group that met on a regular basis. More age specific workshops for young people that ran at regular weekly or monthly intervals, for example. Gaining trust and providing some discussion time around issues of mixed-heritage identity and continuing to work through the arts, as lead by the group; maintaining a sense of fun, co-operation, creative and social exploration.

The families highly valued having a camp and weekends away. They said they would like to repeat that experience where the whole family could be together and there was something for everyone. The group consistently asked to be able to repeat the camp experience, preferably on an annual basis. It was a supportive environment and accommodated all ages and diverse needs within the community that existed for those short amounts of time. It was an excellent way of strengthening networks outside of organised events.

Is it significant that few young parents attended? Does this age group feel that being in a mixed family is less of an issue? Did they know about the project? How did they view it?

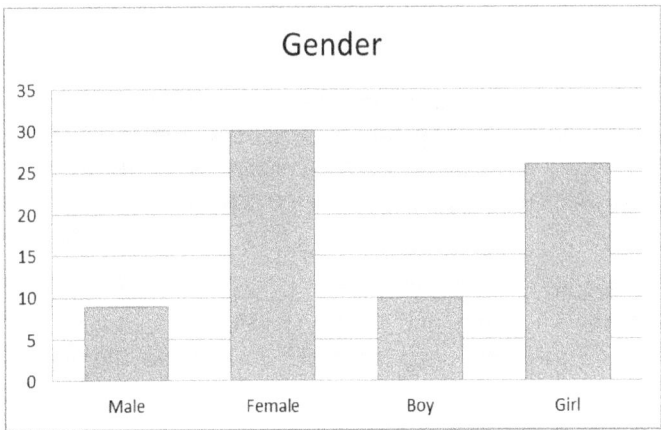

Two thirds more women than men attended this project therefore there were more mothers than fathers present. More girls than boys also attended.

It is known that women tend to participate more in the arts than men do. Why did more mothers than fathers attend? Was there a higher instance of single-parent mothers? Did the mothers bring the children because it was a family oriented activity that fewer men saw themselves as being a comfortable part of?

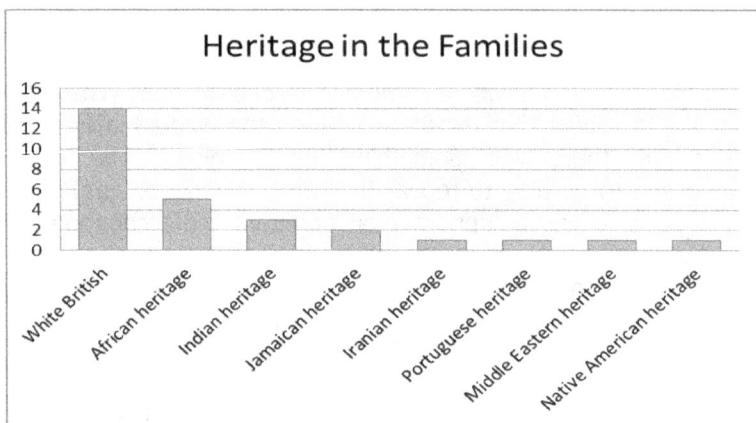

Heritage in the Families

This chart shows the breadth of different cultures and heritages present in the group.

It is a fine example of harmony between people, and also highlights the cultural complexities within a group of mixed-heritage people. It clearly shows that mixed-heritage is not an homogenous group, it cuts across race, culture, religion and skin colour. All the children had one white, or mixed, parent. Some children have more than one other heritage.

Living rurally in Britain the families are surrounded by fantastic opportunities for being in nature and having a wholesome upbringing, but mixed-heritage children and young people do not see themselves reflected back in their communities, especially when it comes to skin colour. As the opening quote shows children in the towns and villages are frequently 'the only one' in their primary school. Mixed children and young people have less opportunity of knowing others in similar circumstances and families must make extra effort for that to happen and for the child, and parent(s), to avoid social isolation. This can sometimes have a knock on effect for the children and young people with self-esteem and confidence. Neither can it be assumed that because people live near natural environments, and could practically access it, does it mean that they do. Poverty and social difficulties can easily be, and frequently are, overlooked in rural areas.

As the majority of mothers on the project were white British with mixed-heritage children then the question arises, "where were the fathers and why were they unable to join their family?" If there were fathers at home why didn't they come? How could they be encouraged, or it be made possible for them to join the family?

If it's a single-parent mother house-hold what kind of cultural role-models are the children and young people getting? How active, or present are the father's in the children's lives? Where are they?

The majority of women who attended the events were white mothers of mixed-heritage children and young people. The majority of men who attended came from ethnic minority backgrounds. There was also consistent participation from ethnic minority mothers and white fathers.

Parminder reported that The Planet Rainbow Project had found a low success rate, over time, in attracting parents from other ethnic groups in a lasting way. They found they did not stay due to the over dominance of white parents; mothers in particular.

One African-Caribbean father who attended some events spoke about how he considered the hardest to reach group to be black fathers. In his opinion he felt they would benefit and provide positive role models for the children, but would not come because they felt it to be a female place, a white cultural space, a victim place where minority groups moan about their experience. He spoke of struggling to get himself along and being aware of cultural and gender barriers to participating, but said that when he was at a Blazing Tales' event with his family he really enjoyed it, felt fine and not emasculated. He found it beneficial for his family to mix with similar families, for him to be present as a role-model and for his child to play with children who had a similar story. He felt that this project was a celebration of mixed-ness and welcoming meeting place for families to get together. It promoted a positive approach to mixed-heritage identity within the context of where they lived.

Each event has left me with a sense of well-being and wanting more. I feel it is an important part of my daughter's sense of self and identity to regularly spend time with other people of mixed-heritage and black/ minority ethnic. We attend various other groups which are almost totally mono culture.

How would you describe your ethnicity?

There was no common way of describing ethnicity and there was a notably individualistic approach to the question. It's a very unpopular question that can make individuals feel boxed and incorrectly represented. What was used here are all different ways of saying the same thing and it's interesting to note how people describe themselves.

These are some examples of typical replies: British Asian English, Anglo-Indian, British Indian – nice skin colour; White/Brown. Half African half English, White & Black – mixed heritage, Global Indian British Gal (G I B G)! White British, British, Physically Caucasian.

Within the array of answers and typical language for mixed-race, there is a localised culture of using the word 'heritage'. This highlights the typical issue facing mixed people and their families of how to describe themselves, as discussed in the introduction.

I tend to say mixed race although the word "race" sticks in my throat because it's a social definition and people see it as scientific. I could never cotton on to mixed heritage because conversely it sounds like you are trying to skirt around something. I try to encourage X... to see himself as mixed rather than black but as he gets older I think he may assume that identify, partly because he is so much darker than the other mixed race kids that he knows.

Another parent said: *I prefer the term mixed-heritage because to say mixed-race implies that we are different races when in fact we are all part of one race - the human race.*

The artist team was well aware of being all white, only able to role-model for the white side of the family and unable to offer other cultural influence with any gravitas. One was a white mother of mixed children. As artists and leaders devising honest and ingenious workshops for the families they were excellent, as can be seen from the reactions and comments. The limits of funding prohibited dropping in artists from other cultural backgrounds and the work under taken during the project by the team was as subtle as the mixed experience and proved to be effective.

If Blazing Tales are able to deepen and develop longer term working with mixed-heritage people, we would put together a more culturally diverse team that better reflected the participants. This project provided valuable learning toward that goal.

The project was not only about diversity, it was also an enquiry into place and working in outside settings. How the arts and stories enliven locations, make lasting memories for the participants and support well-being.

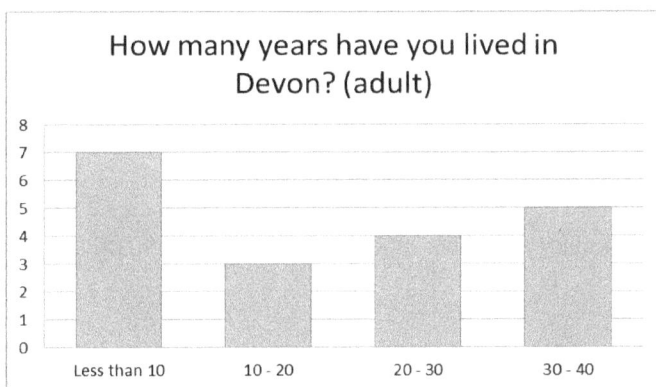

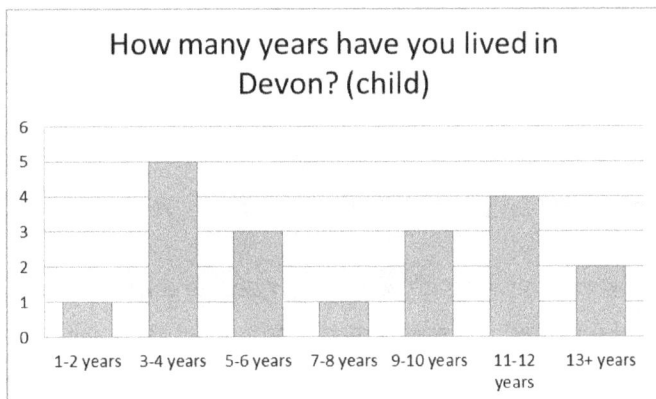

How many years have you lived in Devon? (adult)

	Less than 10	10 - 20	20 - 30	30 - 40
	7	3	4	5

How many years have you lived in Devon? (child)

	1-2 years	3-4 years	5-6 years	7-8 years	9-10 years	11-12 years	13+ years
	1	5	3	1	3	4	2

The majority of adults have lived in Devon for less than 10 years, with the next most common being for 30-40 years which would imply nearly all their lives. However, combined, most adults have lived here for more than 10 years.

Through comparing the adult and child charts it appears that the vast majority of children were born in Devon. They have grown up with the experience of being mixed-heritage, a different skin tone, in a rural setting. It would take a comprehensive study to find out more information about this. How it affects children and young people and how they can be supported.

How did you hear about it?

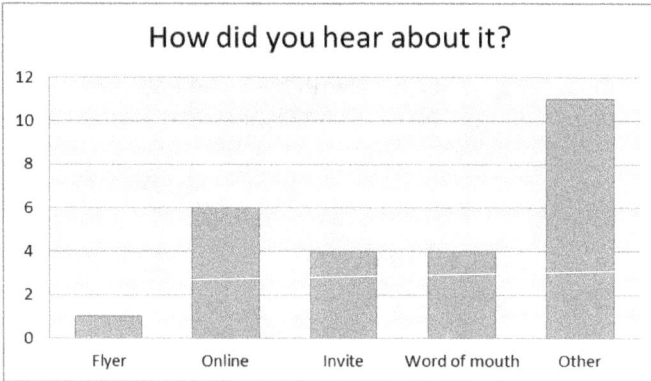

In terms of initial publicity on-line methods were more effective than flyers.

Most people heard about the project by 'other'. Those who had been on previous projects would have already known about this project, and it is estimated that this is the source. No new people came to the last event as the group then existed which skewed the question.

Social

Just being with mixed-heritage families helps to normalise our experience.

So glad not to feel alone and meeting like-minded people is wonderful.

From the charts and repeated comments made throughout the evaluation it is strongly evident that the families, both parents, children and young people found tremendous support in being together. Something extra was found in the exchanges and experience that is not present in their daily lives, which was of enormous value to the majority of families.

How was it being with other mixed-heritage families?

The categories in this question are indistinct and semantically debatable.

This is what the chart looks like if all the similar feelings are put together.

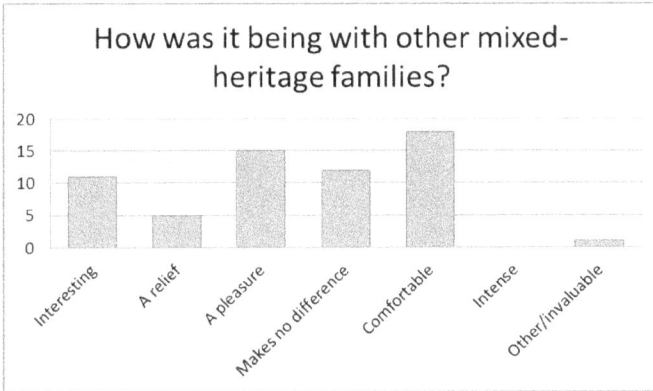

How was it being with other mixed-heritage families?

(Bar chart with categories: Interesting, A relief, A pleasure, Makes no difference, Comfortable, Intense, Other/invaluable)

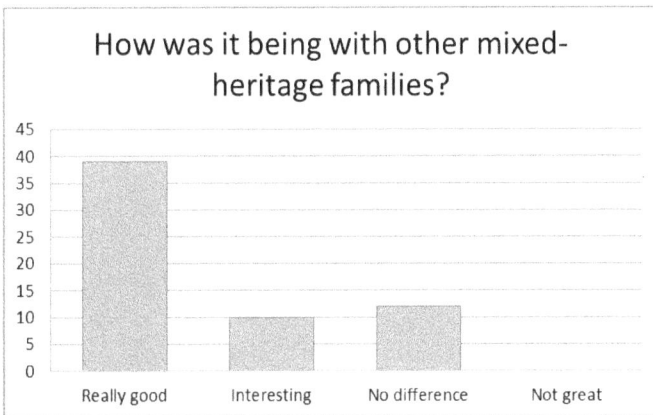

How was it being with other mixed-heritage families?

(Bar chart with categories: Really good, Interesting, No difference, Not great)

People who answered 'it makes no difference to me' made comments like these:

Living in the city we do see other mixed heritage families however to spend time in this environment together is a real encouragement.

Mostly it makes no difference as we find other 'others' but it was great to be in a 'built for purpose' group.

Therefore it was not the fact the event was inconsequential to them. A much needed social opportunity was provided where each family member could share experiences and affirm identity. This ranged from overt, verbal and conscious to subtle, non-verbal behaviour depending on age, level of engagement or ease with the subject of mixed-ness. The mixed-heritage parenting conversations constantly occurred between

171

participants and the non-verbal level the children communicated at was observed through an indefinable sense of relief and relaxation.

I have really enjoyed spending time with my family and mixing with other families.

Could talk about things unselfconsciously - good and bad things about living in dual/mixed heritage families.

Providing an affordable residential or day event for families gave them valuable time together. Neither parent nor child was stressed by separation and all family members had an opportunity to find what they need socially, environmentally, creatively and through the support of other peers. It was observed that all ages formed peer groups and few families naturally stuck together to work as a unit. Provision like this allows for difference of family dynamics and for children and young people to go where they feel comfortable.

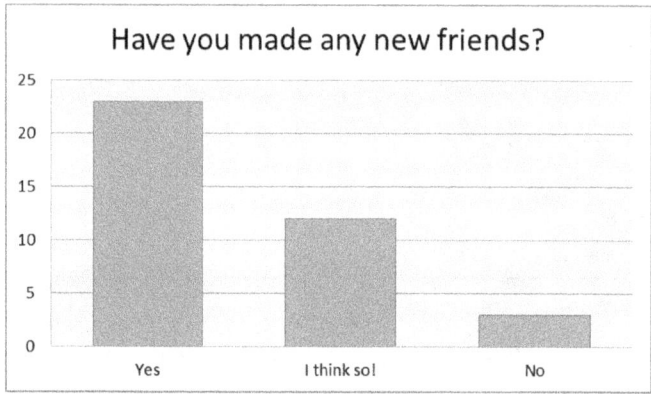

Have you made any new friends?

Yes	23
I think so!	12
No	3

New friendships were clearly formed and new families integrated well with those that knew each other. 'I think so's' tended to be modest, and 'no's' were from those who knew each other.

It was good to see the children building relationships with others like themselves.

I feel it has been a real confidence builder for my children to spend time with other children from similar backgrounds.

Was it a change from your usual experience of living in Devon?

The chart shows that by the families being together they had a different experience of living in Devon. Further detail about this is found in the event sections.

All my family grew up in W. Yorks so were always in mixed heritage groups at school and found it quite a change arriving in Devon.

To re-iterate, this is not intended as either a positive or a negative statement. The families 'usual experience of living in Devon' was one where: it was difficult to meet with families like their own; to meaningfully access the cultures present within their mixed heritage family; or to see them represented around them.

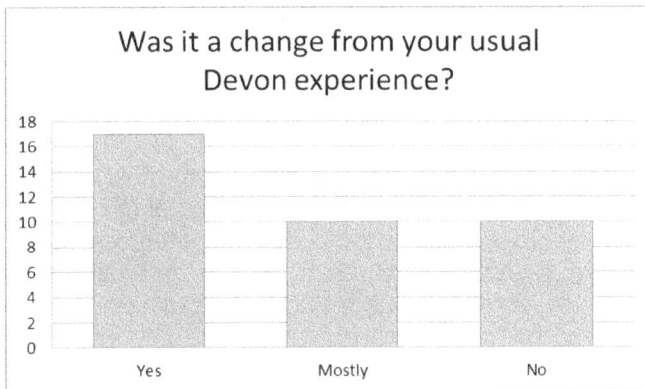

Was it a change from your usual Devon experience?

Devon is one of the biggest counties in the U.K. made up of hundreds of market towns and villages with a very scattered and isolated mixed population. Rural areas tend to have a more static population and, as we found, many of the families had at least one parent who had lived in the county for more than 30 years and whose children were born there.

Our main focus was on strengthening the identity and reducing the social isolation of the children and young people within the family unit. It was not to criticise the area for 'being white' or to assume that this implies it is more or less racist than anywhere else. However, it is certainly true that rurality masks the impact of social exclusion and racism among small, scattered BME populations. (Race Equality in the South West. 2013). The project celebrated Devon's local distinctiveness, it's fabulous countryside, rich history and good way of life, in order to encourage and embed a keener sense of belonging to where you live.

How has exploring Devon affected you?

(chart showing approximate values: More connected ≈14, Nothing new ≈3, Know more ≈23, Will explore more ≈25, Prefer towns/country ≈3, Other ≈1; y-axis 0 to 30)

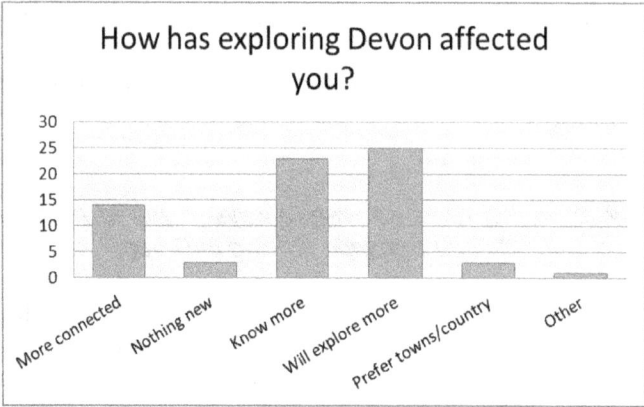

I feel it is so important my daughter feels she has a connectedness with Devon as well as the connections with Jamaica, Nigeria and London.

Good to discover new bits of Exeter & history that I didn't know about.

The chart shows that one of the project aims of knowing more about where you live and encouraging deeper exploration of Devon has happened successfully. One reason for families from other cultural backgrounds not living in rural areas could be that it is usual to remain in the cities and rarely go to the countryside. Cultural attitudes to the countryside are variable. A gross generalization, however to broad sweep one difference of attitude, for example the British pastoral reverence of 'countryside' as opposed to the reverence of hope 'the city' brings for people who come to live here. Did this trait follow with the Exeter based families? Did they explore their locality? From the answers in this section and conversations that took place it's clear that people do not explore new places within easy reach of home very much and tend to re-visit known places.

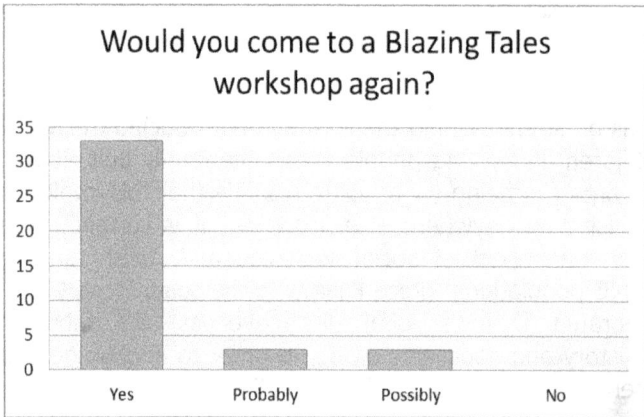

Would you come to a Blazing Tales workshop again?

(chart showing approximate values: Yes ≈33, Probably ≈3, Possibly ≈3, No ≈0; y-axis 0 to 35)

I am very grateful for this experience. Please can we come back again!

PRACTICALITIES

Putting on events for families in the environment means making sure that everyone will be comfortable, safe and looked after enough. Information about what to bring, where they will be, wet weather plans, food and drink plans, and clear organisation are vital to the success of the creative event.

Really enjoyed the whole day – expressing self, history, the tea & cake!

Would you come to a Blazing Tales workshop again?

(Bar chart: Yes ≈ 33, Probably ≈ 3, Possibly ≈ 3, No ≈ 0; vertical axis 0 to 35)

It's important for people to have the information they need for a weekend, or day out, with their families. It improves confidence in the organisation and encourages positive anticipation. This chart shows that everybody was happy with this.

Was the place ….

(Bar chart: Wonderful ≈ 28, Well chosen ≈ 19, Stimulating ≈ 12, Boring 0, Poor 0, Not right 0; vertical axis 0 to 30)

The choices of place were thoroughly enjoyed by people though each one had its drawbacks: wasps, cows, traffic, sea; those draw backs are part of working in outdoor settings, a health and safety check was undertaken at each place and actions implemented. The vitality of each setting was a big part of the project.

Was the food?

Considering they were one-off, outside events, the fact that most people found the food to be 'great' or 'nice' is excellent. Food is an important part of the day when working with families and people's comfort was high on the list. It definitely aids creativity, relationships and good feeling between people!

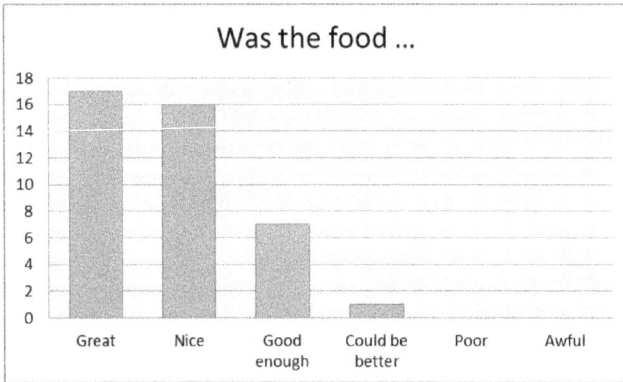

Was the food ...

18	
16	
14	
12	
10	
8	
6	
4	
2	
0	

Great Nice Good enough Could be better Poor Awful

PRACTICALITIES

What did you like the best?
The social side of things was important to the group, and the feeling element of the experience they were having. Parents were also engaging with creativity, able to find their own things that they liked doing, as well as the gratification of seeing their children do it. This follows the aims of the artists to encourage the adults to play, express and create and not to sit on the side and watch their children joining in, or be instrumental in what their children were making or doing. It is also clear from the comments that they did not feel a pressure to join in, but that they actively wanted to and found their own value in it.

What could be better?
There had been one comment made about integrating new children into already intimate friendship groups. We discussed a strategy of giving those familiar young people more responsibility in terms of jobs, and included in that was buddying, and a structure of offering to include others.

THE WORKSHOPS

I liked unwrapping the fabrics, seeing the colours appear, and singing the indigo song while the dipping was happening.

It was the creative arts opportunities that appealed to people to come along. It can be seen from the comments made throughout and charts that the participants learnt new skills and found increased confidence to approach creativity and self-expression. The activities were the back bone of the project.

The art forms of music, visual art and story work are separated for the purposes of the form which does not really represent the close integration and linking of the artists and their work.

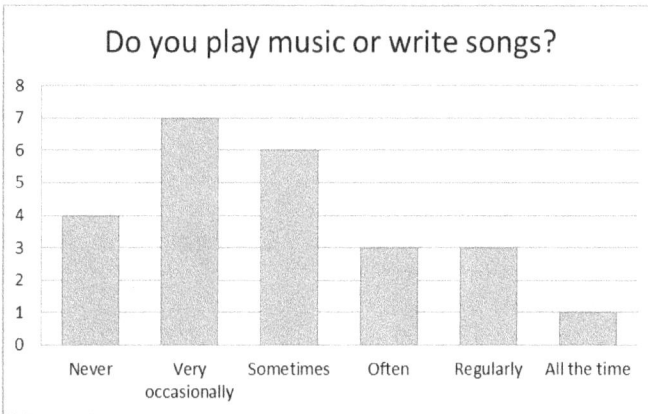

Do you play music or write songs?

From this chart it can be seen that these people do not play instruments or write songs very much, and those that do are most likely competent musicians who play or practise fairly regularly. Does this suggest that this group might lack confidence in their musical abilities, or see it as something for musicians?

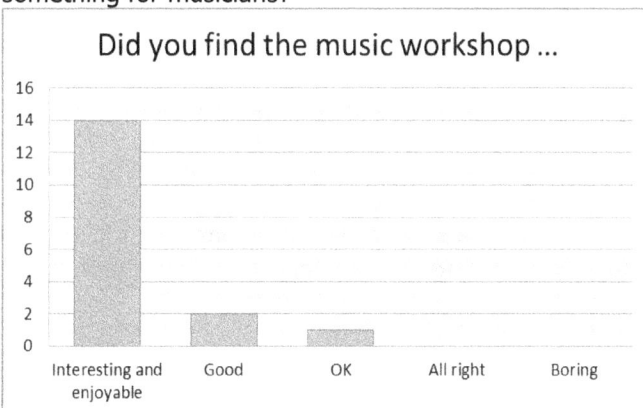

Did you find the music workshop ...

I loved everything about it. The whole event was a big sing song.
What a wonderful way to spend a weekend!
I feel more confident to go about writing a song.
the music wasn't difficult and was open to everybody.

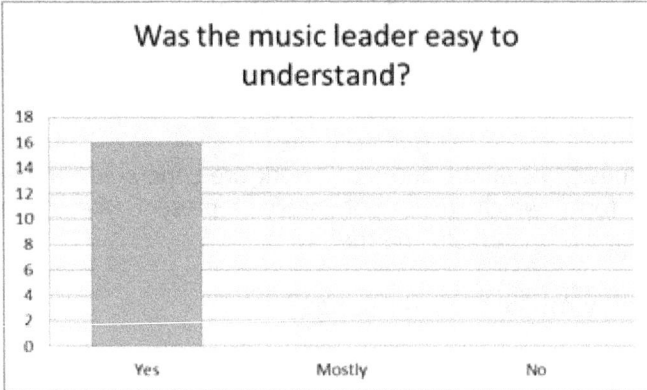

Was the music leader easy to understand?

	Yes	Mostly	No

(Yes ≈ 16)

I enjoy Hugh's workshops and teaching style.
His fluidity, expertise and ease- his cheery, approachable and lively musical character.
He was brilliant with the kids.

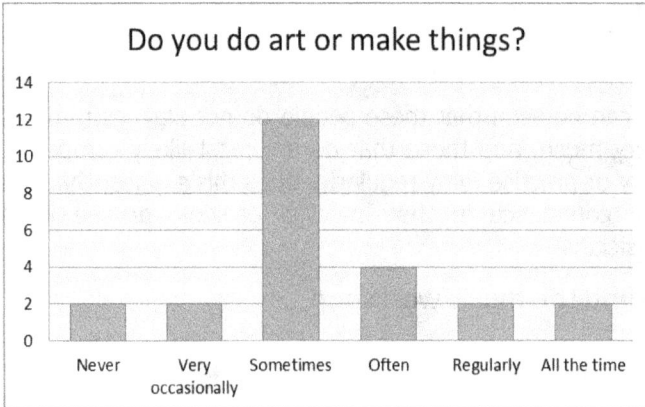

Do you do art or make things?

Never	Very occasionally	Sometimes	Often	Regularly	All the time

(Never ≈ 2, Very occasionally ≈ 2, Sometimes ≈ 12, Often ≈ 4, Regularly ≈ 2, All the time ≈ 2)

This chart is quite a different shape from the music one. Does it suggest more confidence about doing visual art, or that it's more approachable for more people?

I liked drawing and sketching by the river.
Learning how we can use nature around us to be creative.

Did you find the visual art workshop ...

Having a practical art activity running throughout the weekend gives a lovely project to do when you have a spare moment.
Great doing something new, there was no pressure.

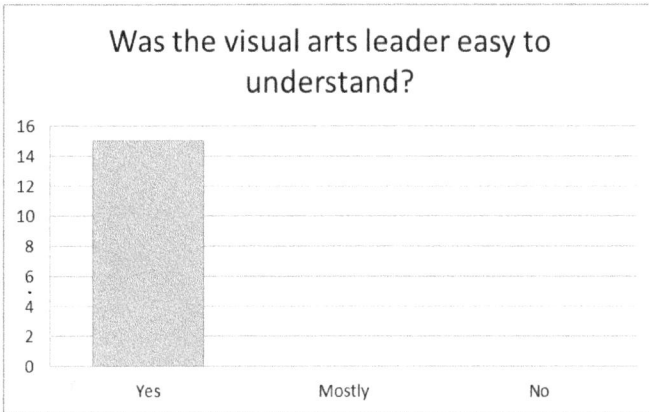

Was the visual arts leader easy to understand?

Cara organised it really well, she was very sharing, and there was space to ask and explore.

Story making and telling

There appears to be a range of difference with making up stories and doing drama; 'very occasionally' and 'regularly' are equal, as are never" and 'all the time.' As sometimes has the most could it be that this is seen as an accessible or common creative activity?

I liked being in the moment and bringing the imagination to life.

Do you do drama or make up stories?

Never	Very occasionally	Sometimes	Often	Regularly	All the time
1	6	8	3	6	1

Did you find the story workshop ...

Interesting and enjoyable	Good	OK	All right	Boring
9	2	3		2

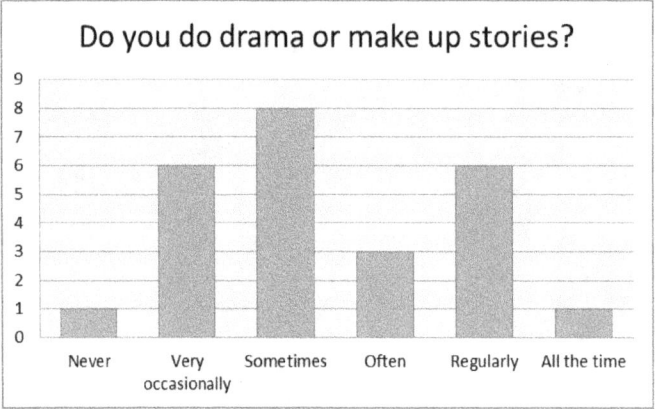

Most people found the story workshop *interesting and enjoyable.*

Hearing the stories making me want to go traveling.

I learnt a lot from talking and listening to others.

Was the leader easy to understand?
The guidance helped me overcome apprehension, I learnt a number of ways to develop and finish an idea.

I liked the storyteller and her skill at it was great.

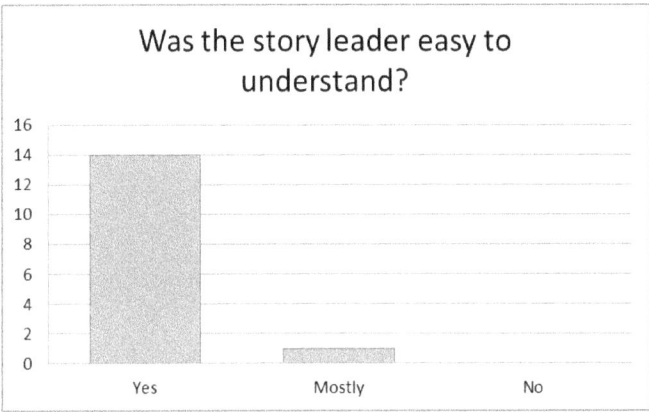

Was the story leader easy to understand?

An integrated approach

The following tables are about the combined arts experience.

I loved the variety – art, music, stories & being outside!

I learnt that you can be inspired by taking walks out in the country side.

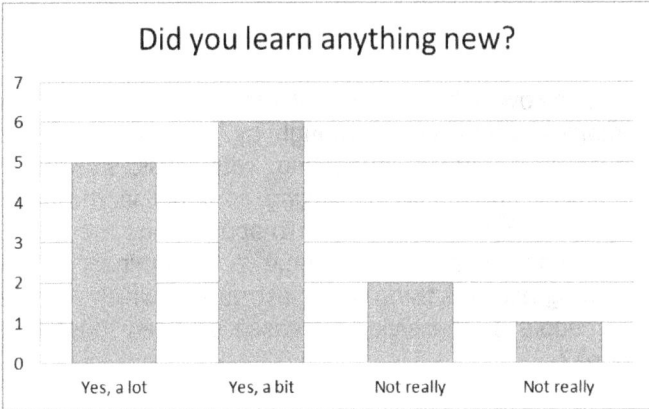

Did you learn anything new?

Did you find all the workshops ...

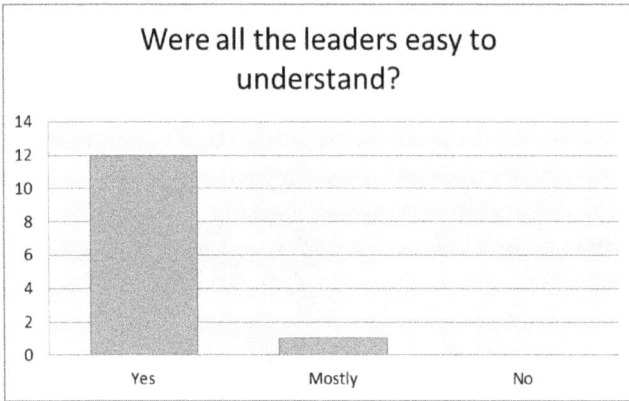

Were all the leaders easy to understand?

A sense of fluidity of leading the days – held & structured, & yet very relaxed.

Collation of responses from under 13's questionnaires.

I would really like to do this more often.

From the three charts below it is evident that many of the under 13's play instruments, make art and stories though by no means all. The different shapes of each art form is interesting, with music showing a different pattern to visual art and story making as it did in the adult charts. Does this represent a different attitude to approaching music and song writing? 'Often, regularly and all the time' are prominent which could suggest the playing and practising of an instrument, which is more common in younger people. Is the divide increased between those that do and those that don't?

Hugh's inclusive approach to music that makes it accessible and do-able by everyone helps to level this playing field and gives everyone a chance to participate, explore, make and enjoy music. However it takes a competent musician and workshop leader to be able to extend that opportunity.

'Sometimes' is prominent with visual art and story and much less so with music. Are making stories and doing visual art easier to approach and find gratification in, something that can be picked and put down more casually than an instrument?

I learnt about making songs out of words.

I enjoyed playing the instruments and trying different ones.

We got to sing.

Joining in. It was fun.

Do you play an instrument outside of school?

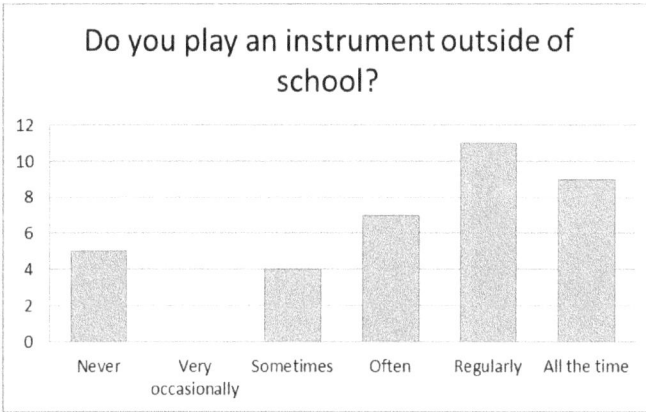

I liked making my bag.

I learnt about waxing and dyeing fabric, about the Indigo dyes and drilling holes in wood to make buttons.

I learnt about sketching with my left hand.

How to make sculpture out of things that you find on a beach and other places.

Do you do art or make things out of school?

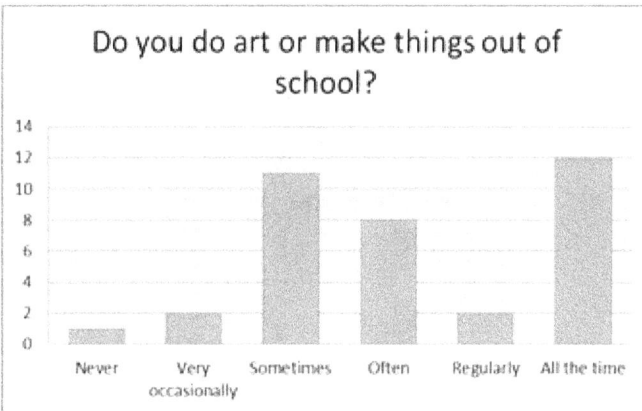

I liked the story about the girl with the horrible step mother.

I liked listening to the stories around the camp fire.

I enjoyed watching everyone's reactions to the stories.

Making up stories on the walk and working together with friends.

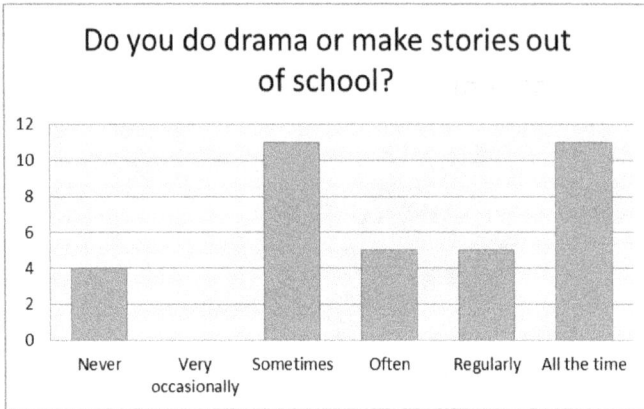

Do you do drama or make stories out of school?

Never	4
Very occasionally	0
Sometimes	11
Often	5
Regularly	5
All the time	11

The following charts show that all the workshops were enjoyed, new things were learnt and the leaders were easy to understand.

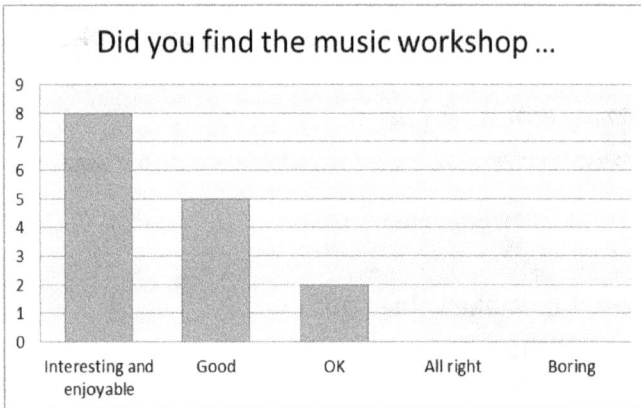

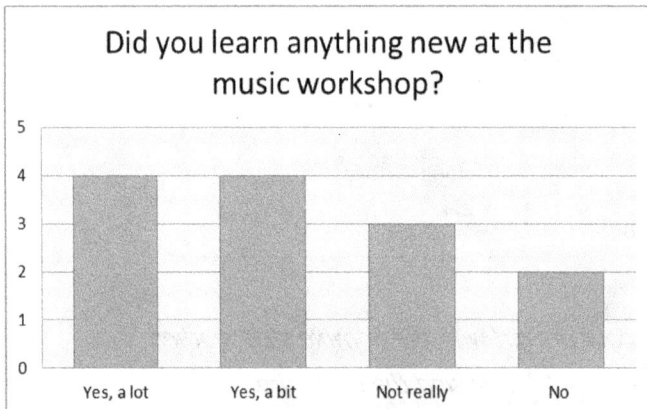

Did you find the music workshop …

Interesting and enjoyable	8
Good	5
OK	2
All right	0
Boring	0

Did you learn anything new at the music workshop?

Yes, a lot	4
Yes, a bit	4
Not really	3
No	2

Was the music leader easy to understand?

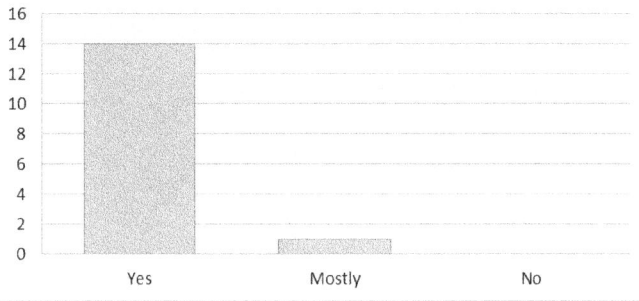

Yes	14
Mostly	1
No	0

Did you find the art workshop ...

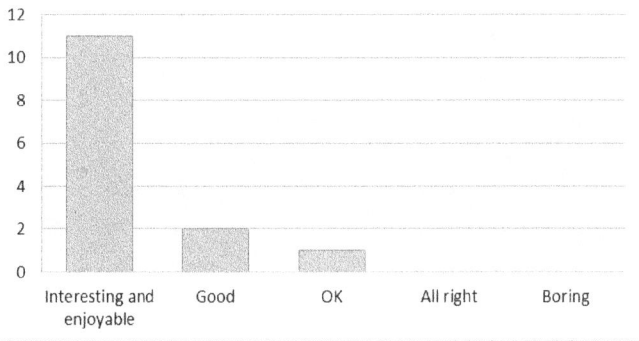

Interesting and enjoyable	11
Good	2
OK	1
All right	0
Boring	0

Did you learn new things at the art workshop?

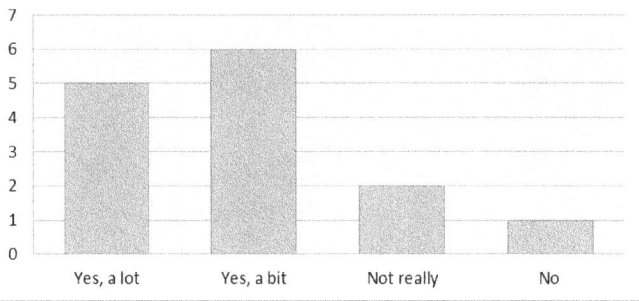

Yes, a lot	5
Yes, a bit	6
Not really	2
No	1

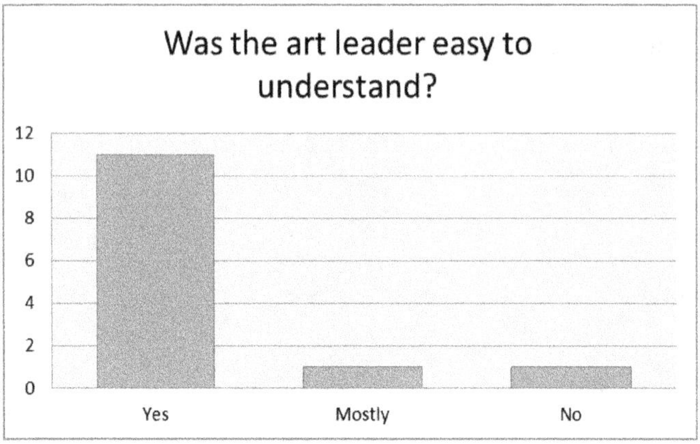
Was the art leader easy to understand?
12
10
8
6
4
2
0
Yes
Mostly
No

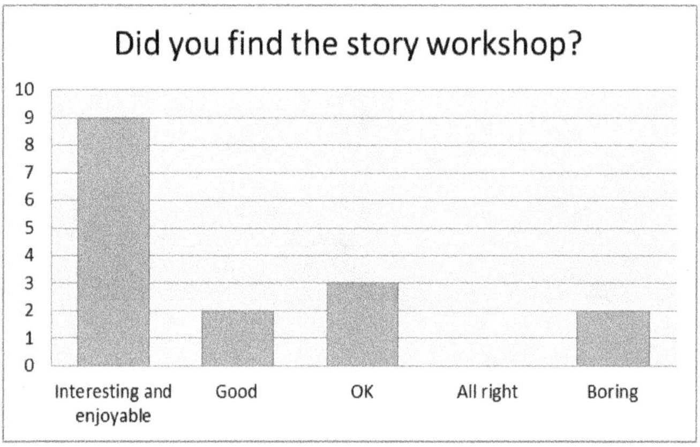
Did you find the story workshop?
10
9
8
7
6
5
4
3
2
1
0
Interesting and enjoyable
Good
OK
All right
Boring

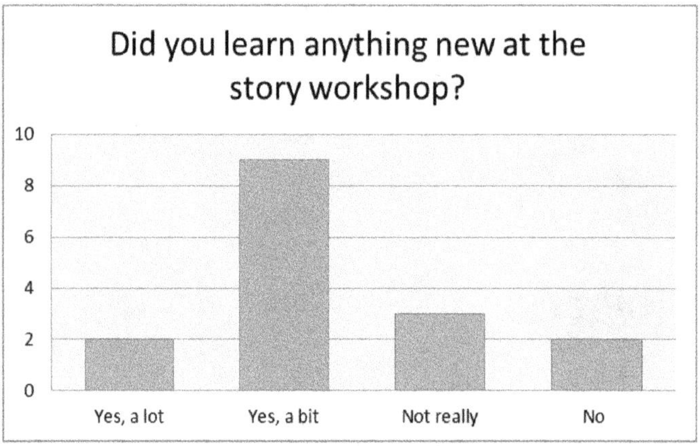
Did you learn anything new at the story workshop?
10
8
6
4
2
0
Yes, a lot
Yes, a bit
Not really
No

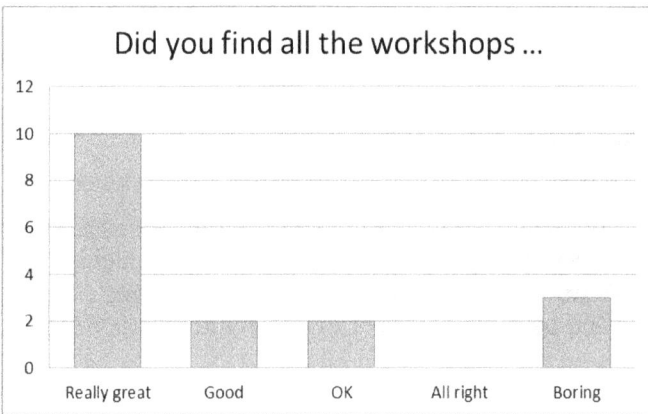

Were all the leaders easy to understand?

Yes	7
Mostly	9
No	1

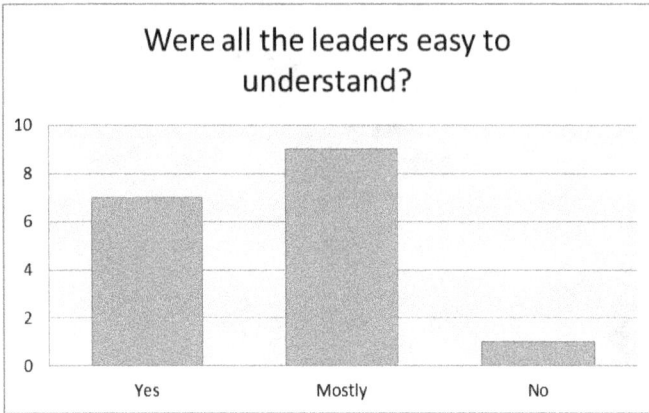

From the comments made by this age group it is possible to see that they developed a greater understanding of the creative process through doing and experiencing.

A real sense of working together and collaboration was shown.

Confidence and ease was increased during the phases of the project.

Looking, listening and finding favoured means of self-expression and making creative connections have been fostered here. It's highly likely that these under 13's would find it easier to do it for themselves after the project has finished and be more confident to join in future opportunities.

Evaluating Wellbeing

The Warwick-Edinburgh Mental Well-being Scale (WEMWBS) is a scale of 14 positively worded items, intended to assess a population's mental wellbeing. The Scale was commissioned at Warwick and Edinburgh Universities in 2006.

Assessing positive mental health requires validated scales which reflect current concepts of mental wellbeing. The 'river exe-pedition' used some of the WEMWBS questions in an informal way to explore the responses and feelings of the families participating.

WEMWBS was developed for use as a population based measure of mental wellbeing and is designed to monitor the mental wellbeing of groups of people over time, especially before and after interventions or programmes. Changes over time can be assessed by examining differences in the mean scores.

The scale had not been validated for use at the individual level when used in the 'river exe-pedition', however individual questions from WEMWBS were being used as triggers for conversations in the context of qualitative research and to guide focus groups etc. They have also been used in the context of 'health promotion projects'. This approach is generally well received but has not been formally evaluated. The number of participants in a study determines the size of the difference which can be said to be statistically significant.

For the purposes of the small numbers involved in the 'river exe-pedition' eleven of the fourteen questions were used and no claim to statistical significance is made.

Since the 'river exe-pedition' concluded the WEMWBS scale is being used as a Wellbeing self-assessment tool through NHS choices. The on line scale scores responses, gives basic advice and suggests useful ways to improve wellbeing. See: http://www.nhs.uk/Tools/Pages/Wellbeing-self-assessment.aspx

Karen Huckvale.

High Exe Valley Weekend

Adult and young people's responses

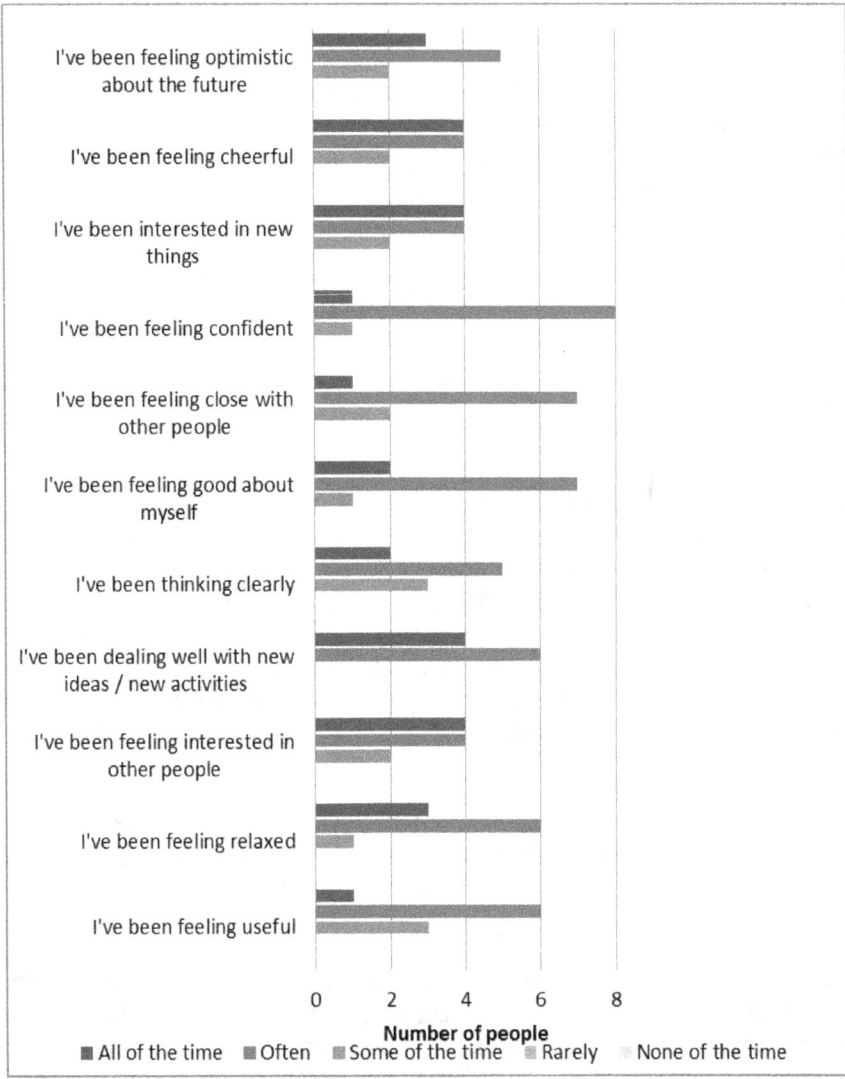

I've been feeling optimistic about the future
I've been feeling cheerful
I've been interested in new things
I've been feeling confident
I've been feeling close with other people
I've been feeling good about myself
I've been thinking clearly
I've been dealing well with new ideas / new activities
I've been feeling interested in other people
I've been feeling relaxed
I've been feeling useful

0   2   4   6   8

Number of people

■ All of the time   ■ Often   ■ Some of the time   ▨ Rarely   ▧ None of the time

High Exe Valley Weekend.

Under 13's responses

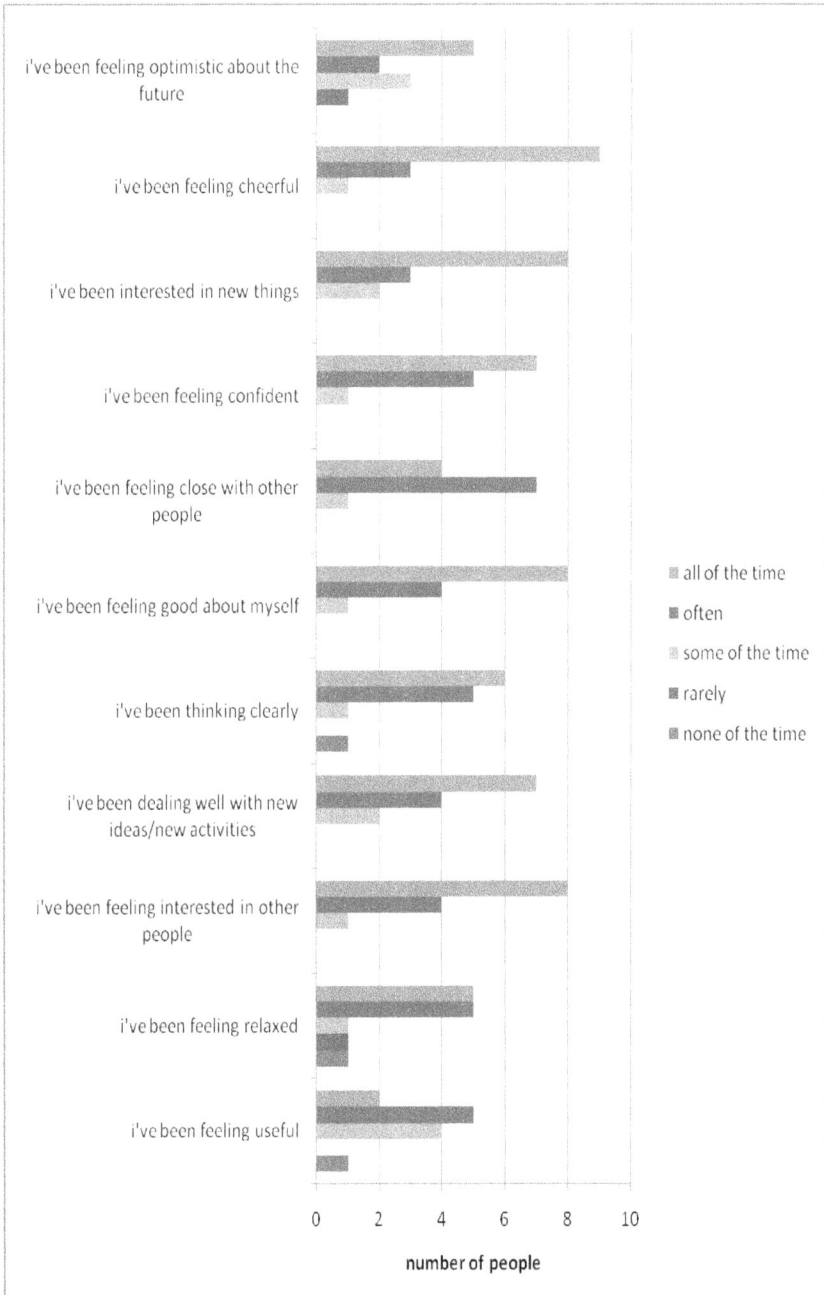

River Bank Day

Adult and young people's responses

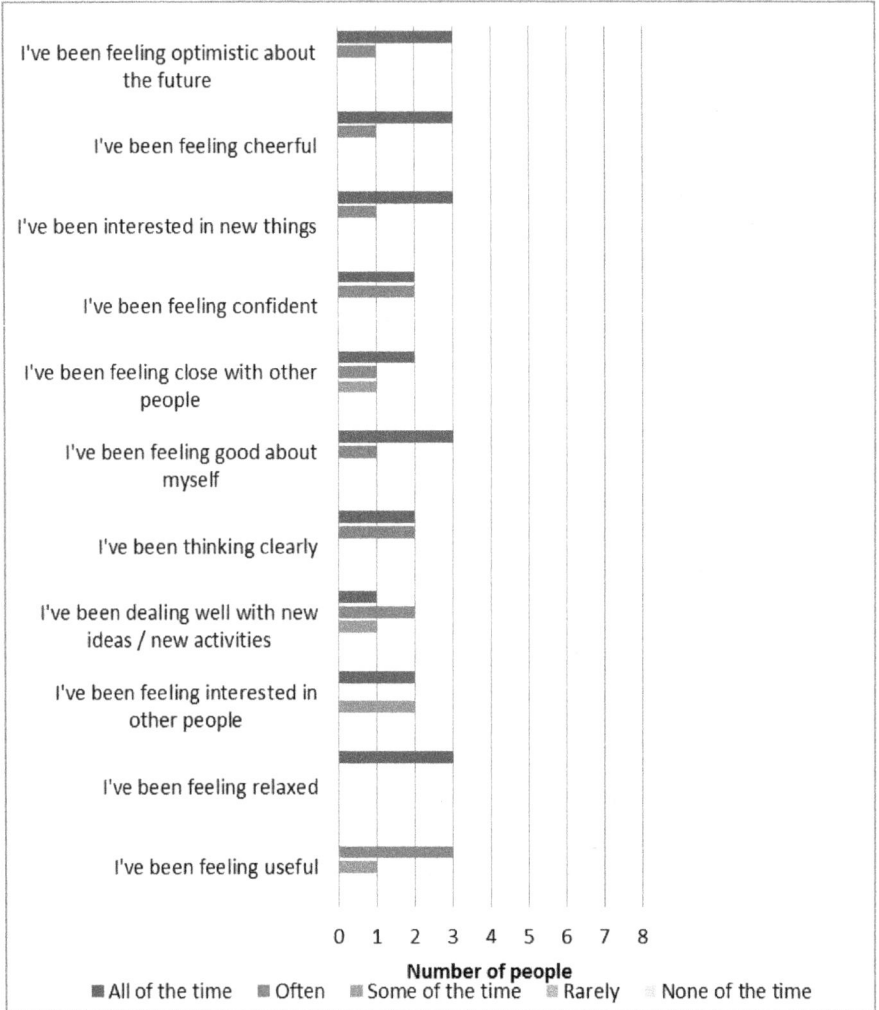

Horizontal bar chart with categories (top to bottom): I've been feeling optimistic about the future; I've been feeling cheerful; I've been interested in new things; I've been feeling confident; I've been feeling close with other people; I've been feeling good about myself; I've been thinking clearly; I've been dealing well with new ideas / new activities; I've been feeling interested in other people; I've been feeling relaxed; I've been feeling useful.

X-axis: Number of people (0 1 2 3 4 5 6 7 8)

Legend: All of the time; Often; Some of the time; Rarely; None of the time

River Bank Day

Under 13's responses

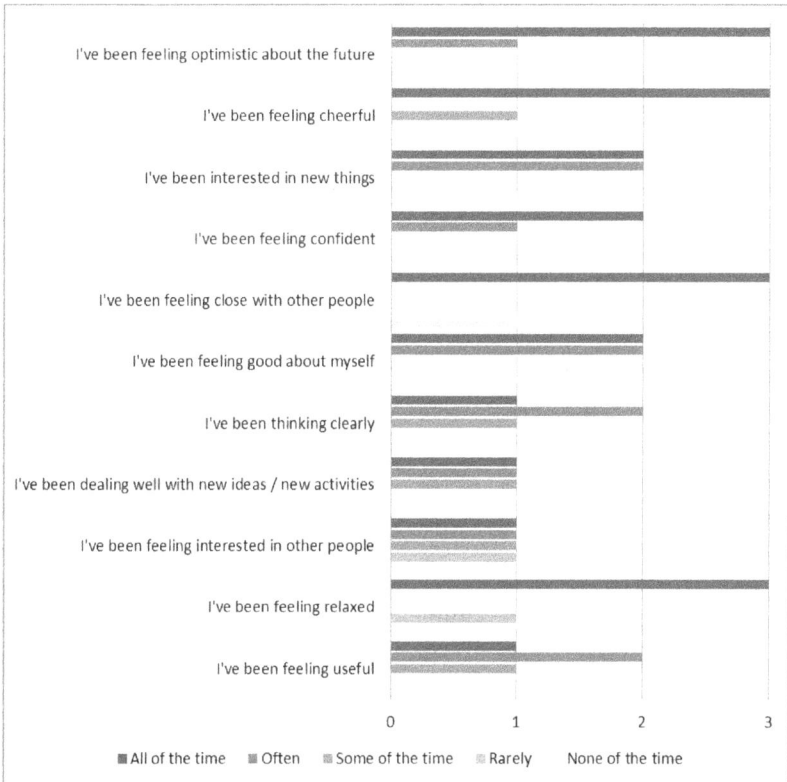

	All of the time	Often	Some of the time	Rarely	None of the time

- I've been feeling optimistic about the future
- I've been feeling cheerful
- I've been interested in new things
- I've been feeling confident
- I've been feeling close with other people
- I've been feeling good about myself
- I've been thinking clearly
- I've been dealing well with new ideas / new activities
- I've been feeling interested in other people
- I've been feeling relaxed
- I've been feeling useful

Exeter

Adult and young people's responses

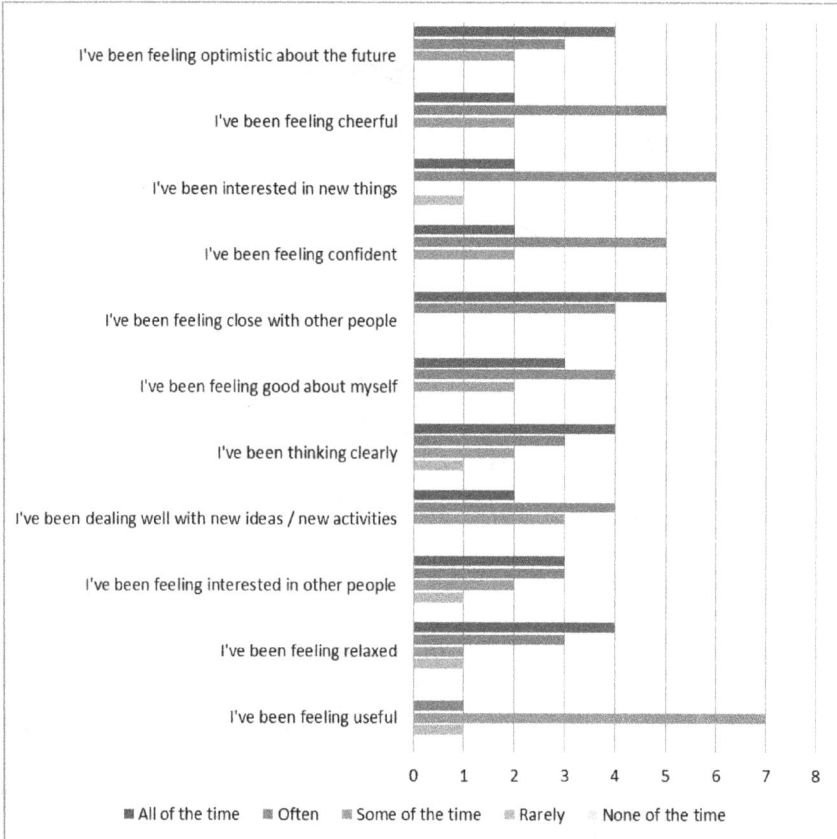

Chart showing responses for the following categories:

- I've been feeling optimistic about the future
- I've been feeling cheerful
- I've been interested in new things
- I've been feeling confident
- I've been feeling close with other people
- I've been feeling good about myself
- I've been thinking clearly
- I've been dealing well with new ideas / new activities
- I've been feeling interested in other people
- I've been feeling relaxed
- I've been feeling useful

Horizontal axis: 0 1 2 3 4 5 6 7 8

Legend: ■ All of the time ■ Often ■ Some of the time ■ Rarely ■ None of the time

Exmouth

Adult and young people's responses

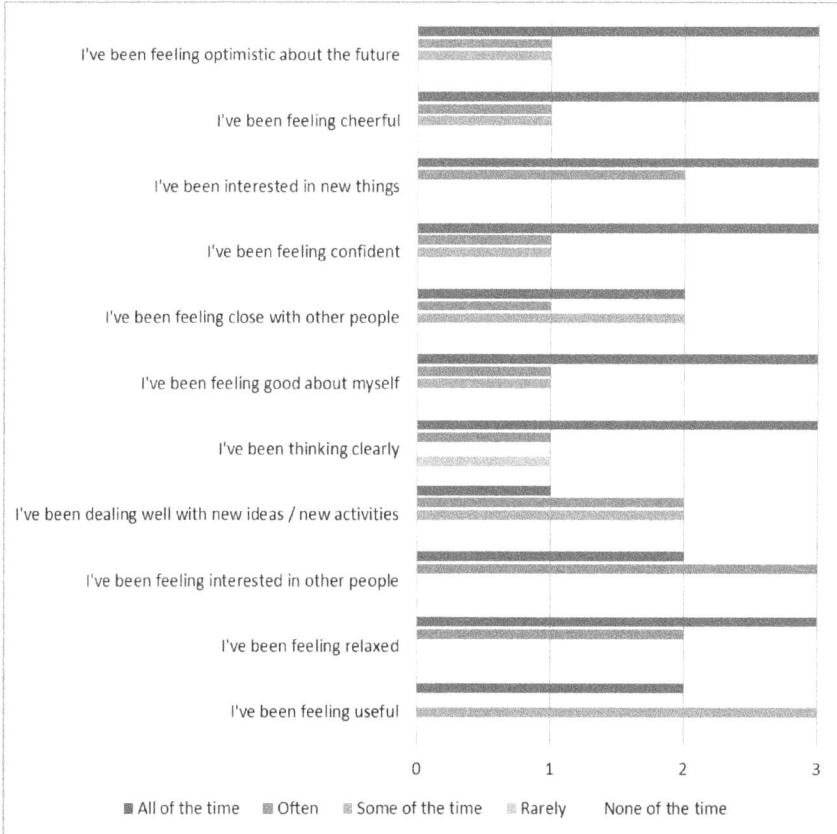

Bar chart showing responses for the following statements:

- I've been feeling optimistic about the future
- I've been feeling cheerful
- I've been interested in new things
- I've been feeling confident
- I've been feeling close with other people
- I've been feeling good about myself
- I've been thinking clearly
- I've been dealing well with new ideas / new activities
- I've been feeling interested in other people
- I've been feeling relaxed
- I've been feeling useful

Legend: ■ All of the time ■ Often ■ Some of the time ■ Rarely None of the time

Exmouth

Under 13's responses

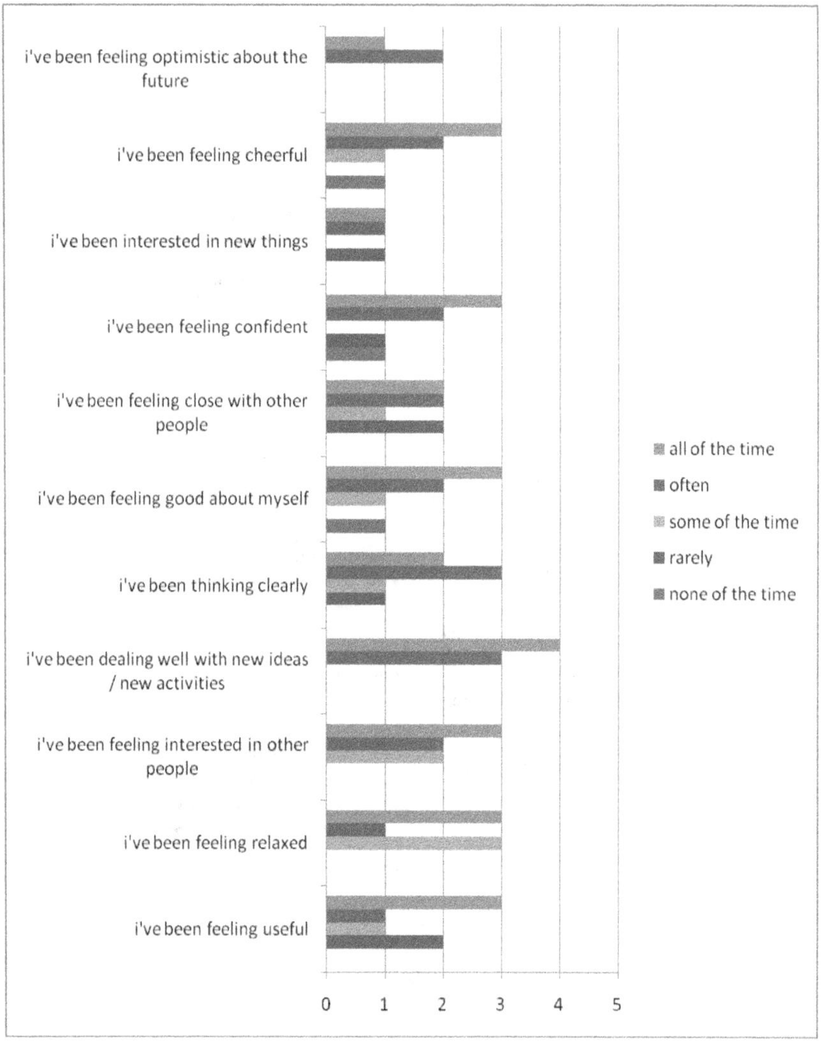

i've been feeling optimistic about the future
i've been feeling cheerful
i've been interested in new things
i've been feeling confident
i've been feeling close with other people
i've been feeling good about myself
i've been thinking clearly
i've been dealing well with new ideas / new activities
i've been feeling interested in other people
i've been feeling relaxed
i've been feeling useful
0
1
2
3
4
5
all of the time
often
some of the time
rarely
none of the time

Conclusion

It is evident that the group became more relaxed with the creative process and expressing themselves as the project progressed. As confidence in participating increased so did willingness to participate in arts activities outside of the project. The change in tone from the beginning to the end of the project shows an increased confidence to approach the arts in the future.

The creative choices the artists made about working site-specifically with their themes worked with the metaphor of the river. The newness at the beginning, entering an unknown creative flow with new people showed itself in the early negotiation of friendship with the young people, improving understanding between families, willingness to engage in the arts and the parent's pressing desire to share stories and talk.

By the last session we had to factor in catch-up conversation and play time because everyone was happy to see each other again and we respected the value of their relationships. The intensity at the beginning had dissolved and become more relaxed as the river flowed into the sea. The group now knew how the artists worked and what to expect. By providing a consistent style of facilitation and workshop flow the participants had grown to trust the artists and their part in the creative process. The families positively anticipated the activities of the day without nervousness.

The choice of working with the subtle themes of mixedness had been fully experienced and understood. The artists had tried to reference most of the cultures of the families attending. From the Exe Valley where the dyeing skills of locally sourced plant dyes picked on the site had been learnt alongside various indigo dyeing techniques. We moved on to the lower Exe Valley near Exeter where we put a 'crocodile' in the River Exe and played gongs alongside the church bells. In Exeter we made 'identity cards' from personal stories, name songs and self-portraits and learnt about the movement of people and river trade across the ages. Finally in Exmouth we went onto the river, joining it on a boat as it ran out into the estuary and the last act of giving the garland of flowers to the sea.

Punctuated along the way with the groups own song compositions, poetry and stories from Britain and around the world which helped to inform a new way of looking at the world close to where we live. Every area has its own local distinctiveness to explore, creatively interpret and celebrate and we chose to take our expedition along the River Exe in Devon. The layers of knowledge, learning, experience and social connection inter-mingled and flowed along the course of the river journey. Is this just a soft outcome? In some ways, yes, there are countless 'positive intangibles' and 'soft outcomes' in this project. I would argue that for the mixed-heritage children and young people living rurally the experience, and its lasting memories, will continue to strengthen their identities and sense of belonging to where they live and nurture broad horizons of a wider world of which their story plays it's part. A world in which these 'third culture kids' are more confident and better able to negotiate their transitions between worlds. Better able too, to stay rooted when faced with discrimination and say like Louise Adjoa Parker "I live here, I belong here, she is mine."

The increase in confidence and self-esteem in the mixed children will stand them in good stead through their education and in social situations. A point of reference has been made and network presented to them which could alleviate feelings of social isolation in the future. When many mixed-heritage children and young people find themselves as the lone brown face in the rural classroom or school these support systems are invaluable - as the families told us many times over. Lasting bonds of friendship between many of the families, individual adults and children were made during this project. As subtle as the experience of living and mixed-ness is, so the subtle choices a person makes can have big impacts on their life.

For the families as a whole the 'river exe-pedition' provided a necessary service and meeting place. This project came out of years of work done by an organisation for mixed families. Without the building blocks of professional networks and awareness raising they had built up this project would have been made more difficult. Mixed-heritage children and young people living in rural areas do face issues specific to them and the psychology is highly complex. With no service provided specifically for them in the community, or much awareness raising in the education system, there are many who will, and do, meet crisis later in life.

This is not a comprehensive or rigorous study, it was a participatory arts project that has shed a little light on one of Britain's quieter issues. There are always limitations, and within the ones Blazing Tales had, we created an intelligent and inventive project for the mixed families of Devon. Resources and partnerships were found and made that could deepen and develop the work further, especially for the children and young people.

We hope the 'river exe-pedition' will open up the debate and get a conversation flowing that can lead to more research, arts based outside projects and further support for rurally based mixed-heritage families. This modest project has shown that engaging in the arts with guidance from experienced participatory arts facilitators is an effective way of supporting children and young people to develop and grow in positive ways. Ways that can continue to sustain them to lead happier, better integrated lives with the self-esteem to help them make choices to support their progress through life. Working in outside settings and creatively exploring places with a leaning towards hidden histories helps to make vibrant memories. Memories that become part of the narrative from which we shape the stories of our lives.

Reflections from the River...
By Katie Grant

indigo
still bruised
our sky
naturally dipped
colour ceases to matter

with common chatter
we trip into evening
ignited
fire eyes stare
reflecting smiles

no one is beyond
too far
in halcyon green
past dreams
laid to rest

testing
brown boy
lost in time
expectations
deserted

in gully deep
classless
our canvases
weave together
shelter

by dawn
smoking
the embers of past
gently turn
in their sleep

new babes
waking
we ascend
into rainbow -
cloudburst

(included with the kind permission of the author.)

Bibliography

Preface

1. J.R.R. Tolkien, *The Fellowship of the Ring*

2. David Pollock & Ruth Van Reken. *Third Culture Kids*. Nicholas Brealey Publishing. UK. 1999

3. Jeremy Holmes. *John Bowlby and Attachment Theory*. Routledge. 1993

4. Barack Obama.: *"Remarks at Southern New Hampshire University Commencement,"* May 19, 2007. Online by Gerhard Peters and John T. Woolley, The American Presidency Project. Retrieved - 2013- from: http://www.presidency.ucsb.edu/ws/?pid=76991

Velvet Dresses

1. Louisa Adjoa Parker. *Salt-sweat and Tears*. Cinnamon Press. North Wales. 2007.

Introduction

1. Sara Hurley's chapter – 'A Riverside Journey' - in *Storytelling for a Greener World*. Edited by E.L. Schieffelin. A. Gersie and A. Nanson. Hawthorn Press. 2014.

2. Arts Council England, *Combined arts: achievements, challenges and opportunities*. Consultation paper. 2010

3. Joseph O'Connor & Pat Seymour. *Introducing Neurolinguistic Programming*. Mandala. London. 1990

4. The Black Environment Network. BEN: http://www.ben-network.org.uk

5. L. A. Parker. *Salt-sweat and Tears*. Cinnamon Press. North Wales. 2007.

6. *Storytelling for a Greener World*. Edited by E.L. Schieffelin. A. Gersie and A. Nanson. Hawthorn Press. 2014.

7. Benjamin Zephaniah. *Too Black, Too Strong*. Bloodaxe Books Ltd; First Thus edition 2001

8. Jo Schofield and Fiona Danks. *Run Wild!* Frances Lincoln. 2011.

9. National Trust. *Natural Childhood Report*. 2012

10. Planet Rainbow leaflet 2007 (out of print)

11. Bradley Lincoln. Mix-d. http://www.mix-d.org 2011

12. Dr Chamion Caballero. R. Edwards. *Lone Mothers of children from Mixed Racial or Ethnic Backgrounds. A Case Study*. Runnymede Trust. London. 2010

13. Peter J Aspinall. *'Mixed race', 'mixed origins' or what? Generic terminology for the multiple racial/ethnic group population*. Anthropology Today. 2009

14. The Office for National Statistics. www.statistics.gov.uk 2011

15.   Dr Chamion Caballero, *Mixed families: assumptions and new approaches. In: Mixed Heritage – Identity, Policy and Practice.* Edited Jessica Mai Sims. Runneymede Trust. London. 2007

16.   Race Equality in the South West: Time for Action. Sept 2013. Paper. Retrieved from www.equalitysouthwest.org.uk

17.   Benjamin Zephaniah retrieved from: www.benjaminzephaniah.com part of a review for the book 'Chinese Whispers' by Hsiao-Hung Pai. 2008.

18.   Lemn Sissay, *Whale Translation.* Retrieved from: blog.lemnsissay.com/2013/06/28/whale-translation/

19.   Sylvia L. Collicott. *Connections.* Haringey. Local-National-World Links. Haringey Community Information Service 1986

20.   W.G. Hoskins. *Devon*. David and Charles Ltd. 1954

21.   Todd Gray. *Remarkable Women of Devon.* The Mint Press. Exeter. 2009

22.   Richard Doddridge Blackmore. *Lorna Doone: A Romance of Exmoor.* (First published in 1869) Wordsworth Classics. 1997

23.   Lucy MacKeith. *Local Black History, a beginning in Devon.* Archives and Museum of Black Heritage. 2003

24.   Todd Gray, *Black History Project.* Friends of Devon Archives. Devon Records Office. 1999

25.   Topsham Museum and St Nicholas Priory, Exeter. From general information.

26.   Jane Marchand, Dartmoor National Park Authority's Senior Archaeologist. Dartmoor National Park magazine 2013/14

27.   Olaudah Equiano. *The interesting narrative and other writings.* Penguin Classics. 2003

28.   Angelina Osborne. *Equiano's Daughter - The life and times of Joanna Vassa.* Krik Krak 2007.

29.   Arthur Torrington. *The Equiano Society.* From the preface to Osborne's 2007 book above.

30.   Sally Ayres, Community Researcher for the TOSFOR project - *Telling our Stories Finding Our Roots* project being led by Exeter's Global Centre. . Her work is unpublished but cites the following, published, sources:

•   *Telling Our Stories, Finding Our Roots: Exeter's Multi-Coloured History'.* Exeter Global Centre project.

•   Carol Christian and Gladys Plummer. *God and One Redhead: Mary Slessor of Calabar.* 1st ed. London: Hodder & Stoughton Religious, 1970.

•   Jeanette Hardage. *Mary Slessor: Everybody's Mother.* The Lutterworth Press. Cambridge. 2010.

31.   Todd Gray. *The Victorian Under Class of Exeter.* The Mint Press. Exeter. 2001

32. Todd Gray. *Exeter Unveiled*. Mint Press. Exeter. 2003 - Image

33. Iain Fraser. *The Palk Family of Haldon House and Torquay*. Sylverwood Publishing. Newton Abbot. 2008)

34. Giles Milton. *White Gold*. Hodder and Stoughton. 2004

35. V. Day Sharman. *Folk Tales of Devon*. Thomas Nelson and Sons. 1952

36. Hugh Lupton. *The Dreaming of Place. Storytelling and Landscape.* Oracle series, Society for Storytelling Press. 2007

37. Alida Gersie. *Storytelling Stories and Place*. Oracle series, Society for Storytelling Press. 2010

Cara Roxanne's Tale

1. Jenny Balfour-Paul *Indigo: Egyptian Mummies to Blue Jeans*. British Museum. 2011

2. Henri Matisse. Translated S. Hawkes. *Jazz*. George Braziller.1998

River Bank Day

1. T. Robyn Batt. *The Fabrics of Fairytale*. Barefoot Books. 2000

2. Jan Knappert. *Pacific Mythology*. The Aquarian Press. 1992

Sara Hurley's Tale

1. Su Hart. Baka Beyond. Personal correspondence.

2. Martin Cradick. Retrieved -2013- from: www.baka.co.uk

3. Jenny Mosely and Helen Sonnet. *101 Games for Better Behaviour.* LDA Publishers. 2006

Exeter

1. Shaun Gladwell. *Seven Year Line Work*. 3rd -29 Oct 2009. http://spacex.org.uk/exhibitions/shaun-gladwell-seven-year-linework-3-october-29-november-2009/

2. Taffy Thomas and Steve Killick. *Telling Tales. Storytelling as Emotional Literacy.* Educational Printing Services Ltd. 2007.

Phil Smiths Tale

1. Phil Smith. *Mythogeography: a guide to walking sideways*. Triarchy Press, 2010.

Exmouth

1. Todd Gray. *Black History Project. Friends of Devon Archives*. Devon Records Office. 1999

2. Duncan Williamson. *A Thorn in the King's Foot: Folktales of the Scottish Travelling People*. Penguin Folklore Library. 1989.

Evaluation

1. Raymond Anyanwu. *Measuring things we cannot measure*. Retrieved - 2013 - from: http://www.poemhunter.com/raymond-anyanwu

2. H. James Harrington. Retrieved -2013 – from: http://www.goodreads.com/quotes/632992

3. Arts Council England. Retrieved – 2013 – from: http://www.artscouncil.org.uk/selfevaluation/

No man ever steps in the same river twice, for it's not the same river and he's not the same man.

Heraclitus